WRITING FOR THE BBC

A guide for professional and part-time freelance writers on possible markets for their work within the British Broadcasting Corporation

Norman Longmate

BBC BOOKS

Norman Longmate is a former member of the staff of the BBC who is now a full-time freelance writer. While employed by the BBC he worked as a radio producer and in the BBC Secretariat. He has written a large number of radio and television scripts, specialising in school broadcasting and in historical documentaries. He has also worked as a historical adviser to a number of television programmes and series, including *Nanny*, shown on BBC-1, and the award-winning Yorkshire Television schools series *How We Used to Live*. His books, mainly on nineteenth and twentieth-century social history, especially the civilian side of the Second World War, include the best-selling *If Britain Had Fallen* published by BBC Books and Hutchinson. Norman Longmate is an active member of the Society of Authors and has served on its Broadcasting Committee.

The text of the sections dealing with the requirements of individual parts of the BBC is based on material supplied by the various Regions, Departments and Local Radio Stations listed, whose help is gratefully acknowledged.

While the information given here was correct at the time it was compiled, change in broadcasting is a continuous process. Some of the details, especially concerning individual series, may therefore have altered by the time this booklet is consulted.

Published by BBC Books
a division of BBC Enterprises Limited
Woodlands, 80 Wood Lane, London W12 0TT
First published 1966   Eighth edition 1988

© The British Broadcasting Corporation 1988
ISBN 0 563 20468 0

Set in 10/11 pt Times and printed in Great Britain
by Redwood Burn Ltd, Trowbridge, Wiltshire
Cover printed by Fletchers Ltd

Contents

Introduction

Since it came into existence in 1927 the British Broadcasting Corporation has become by far the largest single patron of the writer, both professional and amateur, in Great Britain. For the professional writer it has provided entirely new opportunities and a new audience, of a size previously undreamed of. Radio and television adaptations of published work have enabled the writer to gain wider recognition, and the specially written radio and television play have now emerged as art forms in their own right, offering new outlets for his talent. Many playwrights who have become well known in the cinema or theatre have first made their name as the authors of television plays and instead of broadcasting being regarded as a rival to other creative media, as tended to happen in its early days, an increasing amount of interchange has taken place between those writing for the stage or screen on the one hand and for the radio loudspeaker and television screen on the other. The serialisation of published books has helped the novelist and the non-fiction writer to make their work known to many who might never buy a book or visit a library, while talks and discussion programmes have given writers the chance to put forward their ideas in public, and to develop an additional source of income to help support them in their hazardous profession.

For the spare-time writer, who combines authorship with some other occupation, radio and television have provided a vast new outlet. Radio alone uses around six hundred plays a year, most of them specially written for broadcasting and many by part-time authors. The BBC provides, too, one of the few remaining outlets for the writer of short stories, a literary form popular with the non-professional writer who is trying to establish himself in his craft.

There is a third group too, for whom radio and, to a lesser extent, television have provided a unique means of self-expression, namely those described as 'kitchen-table writers' who have neither the qualifications nor perhaps the ambition to become professional authors but who feel called on to write about their opinions or experiences once or twice in a year, or a lifetime. They include many house-bound mothers of families and retired people of both sexes, to whom radio in particular has long been a familiar companion. The BBC has helped to give these amateur writers, who might have found no other outlet for their talents, the chance to establish contact with an audience, and to be paid for doing so.

For all three types of writer, the range of opportunities has never been wider. The markets offered by independent television and radio are clearly outside the scope of this booklet, but the hostility which sometimes existed between 'public service' and 'commercial' broadcasting while the latter was still a novelty has now been replaced by a friendly rivalry; having contributed to ITV or ILR is not regarded as a disqualification when approaching the BBC. At the same time the prospect of substantial 'residuals', i.e. amounts earned by a script beyond its original fee, is constantly improving as the BBC develops its commercial arm, BBC Enterprises Ltd, which, with the pegging of future increases in the licence fee to the rate of inflation, has become an increasingly important source of finance for the development of services and the enrichment of programme output.

The opportunities for the sale of radio programmes originated for the domestic services to stations overseas are very limited, though some do exist; but the worldwide market for television is ever-growing. In addition to the sale of programmes for 'theatric' showing, i.e. transmission over foreign and commonwealth television networks, the Home Entertainment side of Enterprises is making more and more programmes available for private purchase and playback. Depending on the terms of his contract with the BBC, the writer receives a share of these additional earnings. The BBC is not itself involved in Direct Broadcasting by Satellite, but the rapidly growing demand from the companies who are engaged in it can only be more beneficial to all who write for television.

The other major development which will occur over the next few years is the increasing use of independent, i.e. outside, producers and production companies as a source of programme supply. The BBC announced in October 1987 that it intends by 1990 to commission up to 600 hours a year of television programmes from outside organisations. The present booklet does not cover the operation of external programme producers, but clearly they present an additional market through which scripts may be broadcast by the BBC though not directly commissioned by it.

The BBC already receives several thousand unsolicited manuscripts a year, comparatively few of which are ever broadcast. Yet many producers are anxious to extend the range of contributors to their programmes and both radio and television use material at such a rate that new ideas, and new names, are always welcome. The reasons why scripts are turned down are often obvious to everyone except their author and, just as in any publisher's or newspaper office, unsolicited contributions which are rejected are always likely to outnumber those which are bought, since most work will be commissioned from contributors already known to the editors responsible. But those with a real urge to write will disregard this discouraging fact, remembering that everyone had to start sometime, and that even the most successful authors often had a series of failures before finally selling the book or play which made their name. The aim of this book is not to stimulate a flood of contributions from people who have never before thought of writing for broadcasting, but to help those who do have the desire to write for broadcasting to avoid some obvious pitfalls and at least to reduce the odds against their selling their work. Surprisingly few intending free-lance writers, for example, ever seem to have made any attempt to understand the organisation of the BBC, although this is obviously important if they are to try to place their work effectively. Even more astonishing is the number of people who submit scripts without specifying for what department they are intended or even with the suggestion that they should be used in television or radio as the BBC thinks fit. The needs of the two media are quite different and if an author does not know for which he is writing his work is almost certainly not suitable for either. It can hardly be stressed too emphatically that it is not the BBC's responsibility to try to find a placing for amateur contributions which the author thinks might somehow merit broadcasting but the writer's obligation to assess the possible outlets and tailor his work to them.

This is not a textbook on how to write for broadcasting; many such publications already exist, some of which are listed as an appendix to this booklet. The BBC does not aim to provide the would-be writer with systematic training but to give him guidance and encouragement. Clearly neither this, nor any, publication, can implant literary talent where it does not already exist. It cannot teach anyone to write. What it can do is to help those who have the ability to write for the BBC.

Some General Advice

By far the most important piece of advice for anyone wishing to write for radio and television is to listen and view as much as possible. BBC radio does not exist to cater for those with a vague feeling that they would like to talk on the air, and BBC television was not created to provide a home for plays which have found no place on the West End stage. Radio and television are distinctive means of communication with their own limitations and possibilities and their own particular techniques, and anyone who seriously wishes to sell his work to the BBC must first make himself familiar with its existing output.

Second, as in every other type of freelance writing, the potential scriptwriter must study his market. There is, for instance, no single type of radio play, for the BBC's large output is broken down into distinctive series, each with their own characteristics. A play will have a far better chance of acceptance if the writer decides in the beginning whether he is, say, writing for a Radio 3 or a Radio 4 audience, and even more if he has in mind a specific series such as *Saturday Night Theatre* or *The Monday Play*.

The same is true of talks. It is not sufficient to decide that one would like to deliver a talk on one's recent holiday. Instead the would-be author must ask himself: 'What Programme is most likely to use material of this sort?'; 'Is there a particular series within that Programme into which it might fit?'; 'Have they used similar, but not too similar, items before?'; and, not least important, 'What length of talk do they prefer?' Similar rules apply to television. The television audience has been studied in great detail, and a television programme is likely to be produced with a particular 'slot' in mind, that is a particular time on a particular day of the week. The audience at 7.00 p.m. on Friday is different from the 9.00 p.m. audience on Saturday, and both are different from the 5.00 p.m. audience on Sunday. The author must not be hypnotised by the varying requirements of specific audiences, but they will certainly be in the mind of the producers and executives who ultimately decide whether or not to buy his work.

An exceptionally common fault, understandable in that so many people first begin to think seriously of writing for the BBC when they have retired and at last have ample leisure to view and listen, is to write about a type of world, or for a type of programme, that no longer exists. It is hard for those past or approaching retirement age to appreciate that the producer considering their script may never even have heard of a programme that once delighted them, but which was last broadcast before he or she was even born. *Grange Hill* is a very different place from Greyfriars; the Ditcham Heath occupied by *Citizens* has little in common with Mrs Dale's Parkwood Hill. Nostalgia, though manifestly not unmarketable, is rarely an encouragement to original thinking; and it is the contemporary world which is of most interest to the majority of viewers and listeners. The atmosphere of *Casualty*, for example, is wholly remote from that of the traditional hospital series; the streets patrolled by *Juliet Bravo* are a harsher place than those once trodden by *Dixon of Dock Green*. Comedy has perhaps changed even more. The central situation of *After Henry*, broadcast on Radio 4, with a middle-class widow burdened with the presence and problems of her elderly mother and grown-up daughter respectively, is one common to any age but the treatment is firmly contemporary.

Just as times have changed, so techniques and fashions in broadcasting alter. In radio, for example, a high proportion of documentaries mainly or wholly consist of linked actuality recordings, and even where (for example in the recent series on *The Crusades*) scripted passages are included they may well be interspersed with on-the-spot recordings. The tape recorder, not the pen, is increasingly the radio writer's chief instrument. Where, as in radio light entertainment and drama, the written word still provides the content, freshness of approach is the quality most likely to arrest the attention of the audience and, what is more important to the writer, of the BBC official who first reads his script. The Lake Poets, for example, hardly sound a promising subject for a radio comedy series, but, thanks to its unconventional, irreverent approach, *The Wordsmiths of Gorsemere* was a great success with listeners and critics alike. As suggested above, the way to find out what works on radio or television, and the type of material which is likely to appeal to producers and network controllers, is to listen and view constantly. For this there is no substitute and accompanying letters which explain that the writer has little time to enjoy programmes or, alternatively, that he or she has tried to produce something better than 'most of the rubbish you put on' do not improve the chances of a script being sympathetically received.

The contributor can also make his task easier by gaining some knowledge of the way in which the BBC is organised. At present scripts sent initially to the wrong department are normally forwarded to the office which is most likely to be interested, but this involves unnecessary delay and may reduce the impact of the script on the producer who reads it when it finally reaches his desk. The relationship between the various production departments, which actually make programmes, and the four radio and two television networks which broadcast them, is explained later in this book. A play with a West Country setting, for example, may have its best chance of acceptance if offered to the BBC Network Production Centre in Bristol, while a talk on the English theatre by a foreigner living in Britain might be of greater potential interest to the External Services than to the domestic ones. It is therefore worth an author's while to familiarise himself with the general pattern of BBC organisation, in order to avoid overlooking the less obvious markets for his work. For this purpose, the *BBC Annual Report and Accounts* is an invaluable source of reference and will supplement the summary which follows

Schools of Journalism and Literary Agents

A writer must clearly decide for himself whether or not he would profit from enrolling with a school of radio and television writing and the BBC is unwilling to advise individuals on this point, or to recommend a particular school. Enrolment with a writing school is, however, generally considered to be of most help to a writer who is weak in the technicalities of writing, particularly for television. Such schools often advertise in the literary magazines. *The Writers' and Artists' Yearbook*, published annually by A. & C. Black and available in most public libraries, contains a great deal of information on relevant subjects, including a list of literary agents. Here, too, the BBC prefers not to advise the individual writer and as a matter of policy it gives equal consideration to work submitted direct by the writer or through an agent. Agents can, however, be very helpful to a writer. They may find for his work a market he had never considered and they are often in touch with individual producers in radio, and with the Script Unit and individual story editors in television.

The Organisation of the BBC

The organisation of the BBC is often confusing to outsiders. This reflects the facts that the BBC has studios or offices in 55 towns and cities throughout the British Isles; employs 24,000 people; and broadcasts, on the national networks alone, some 580 hours of radio each week and some 200 hours of television, in addition to Open University programmes, the extensive output of the National Regions, the Television Regions and the local radio stations. The BBC's programmes range from the most undemanding of light entertainment on BBC-1, attracting audiences of fifteen million, to the most serious cultural programmes on Radio 3, whose listeners may be numbered in thousands. It produces every year far more plays, both new and old, than the entire West End stage and a much greater volume and variety of journalistic news and comment than the whole of Fleet Street. Even a modestly successful radio programme commands a far larger audience than a best-selling book while a feature film shown on television will reach in an evening a far larger audience than it achieved in all the cinemas in the country put together. Total expenditure of the BBC's home services, some £900 million in 1986/87, gives some indication of the scale of its operations.

The domestic services of the BBC consist basically of two television channels, or networks, and four radio networks. ('Network' in BBC terms means the basic service covering the whole of the United Kingdom, as distinct from Regional or Local broadcasts, seen or heard only in one area.) These networks are mainly supplied with programmes by the production departments in London (also sometimes referred to as 'supply' or 'output' departments) but many programmes are also made for transmission on the national networks in the three National Regions and the five English Regions. The nature of the output of both types of Region is described in more detail later. The National Regions transmit a service of their own in place of the BBC-1 service received in England, though most of their programmes are drawn from BBC-1 and the majority of these are broadcast simultaneously. The five English Regions carry BBC-1 but 'opt-out' of it at certain times to transmit their own programmes. These are mainly of a topical, news-orientated nature, but the Regions also produce some features, of which a number are repeated on the national networks. BBC radio, like television, also has a two-tier structure. In addition to the four national networks, covering the whole country, there are thirty-two local radio stations, each serving a single county or community. Each English Region contains a number of local radio stations, the manager of which is initially responsible to the Head of Regional Broadcasting for his Region and ultimately to the Managing Director, Regional Broadcasting, in London. The local stations broadcast their own programmes for part of the day and for the rest of the time they are on the air carrying 'sustaining' material from one of the national networks. Some items from local radio are repeated on one of the networks and, less frequently, whole programmes, while all the local stations contribute when necessary to the BBC's national news-gathering service. Essentially, however, each station serves its own area, and has a distinctive character appropriate to it.

The BBC announced in October 1987 plans for a radical re-organisation in the long-term of its radio frequencies, which may mean, for example, that Radio 4 on long-wave becomes an 'events' network carrying coverage of party conferences and 'running' news stories. These changes will not, however, affect the requirements of the various networks so far as the writer is concerned. The present position is that Radio 4 is transmitted on long wave and FM nationally, and on medium wave in the London area. Radio 3 and all the local stations have both medium wave and FM frequencies. Radio 1 and 2 have separate medium frequencies, while for the most part sharing a single FM outlet. The two networks will have entirely separate FM facilities by 1990, and this has already happened in the London area.

At present, (though, as indicated above, the whole frequency situation will change in the future), the transmitters serving Radio 4 are sometimes split so that it is possible for two different programmes to be carried simultaneously. Thus during school terms, for example, Radio 4 carries school programmes during school hours on FM but general programmes on long wave.

Similar arrangements are made for some Continuing Education (i.e. BBC-originated) and Open University (i.e. Open University produced) programmes and, though splitting the networks can be frustrating to the listener required to retune his set, the result is to increase the amount of airtime to be filled.

The situation in Wales, Scotland and Northern Ireland, known in BBC terms as 'the National Regions', is different from that in England. In place of BBC-1 BBC Wales, BBC Scotland and BBC Northern Ireland provide television services of their own. These are presented from Cardiff, Glasgow and Belfast respectively and consist partly of programmes produced solely for the Region concerned, but mainly of programmes shown on BBC-1. These are mostly transmitted simultaneously, as, for example, in the case of the main United Kingdom news bulletins, but, to accommodate 'opt-out' programmes, a few are moved to different times or may be dropped altogether, although this usually affects repeats, or feature films likely to be shown again. The majority of 'opt-out' programmes made for BBC Wales, BBC Scotland and BBC Northern Ireland are not seen in other parts of the United Kingdom, although some may later be transmitted on one of the national networks. BBC Wales now 'opts out' of about seven hours of BBC-1 each week, BBC Scotland out of about ten hours, and BBC Northern Ireland out of about seven hours, although in each case about two and a half hours is accounted for by the regional news magazines.

In the case of radio, the listener virtually everywhere has a choice between Radio 4 UK or long wave (i.e. the 'basic' Radio 4 network service presented from London) and a Regional radio service. In Wales, in addition to Radio 4 UK on long wave, Radio Wales, produced in Wales for the English-speaking audience, is available on medium wave, and Radio Cymru, in the Welsh language, on FM. In Scotland, Radio 4 is available on long wave, except in a very few places, and Radio Scotland can be heard on medium wave and FM. In Northern Ireland Radio 4 is available on both medium wave and long wave, while Radio Ulster can be heard on both medium wave and FM. This latter consists partly of programmes made in, and for, that province and partly of material taken from other BBC radio networks.

BBC Management

The highest authority in the BBC consists of the Board of Governors, under the Chairman and Vice-Chairman. The Governors are appointed by the Queen in Council, which in practice means on the advice of the Prime Minister of the day. They are normally part-time appointments, although the chairman devotes most of his time to BBC business. The Governors are not concerned with the day-to-day control of the BBC's affairs. This is the responsibility of the chief executive of the BBC, and its senior full-time official, the Director-General. The Director-General presides over the BBC's Board of Management, which meets every week and consists of the Directors in charge of Personnel, Finance, Engineering and Corporate Affairs, the four Managing Directors, for Television, Network Radio, Regional Broadcasting and External Broadcasting, the Director of Programmes Television and the Deputy Director-General, who is responsible, under the Director-General, for the BBC's News and Current Affairs output. The Managing Director, Regional Broadcasting, is responsible for both radio and television output within the Regions, National and English, including local radio. The Managing Director, External Broadcasting, is assisted by a Deputy Managing Director, who is not a member of the Board of Management. Apart from his more general responsibilities, he is particularly concerned with the BBC World Service, in English, and the central departments which provide material in English for use usually in translation by the various services directed, in their own languages, towards particular countries or parts of the globe. These are organised under two Controllers, for European Services and Overseas Services respectively.

Although the External Services transmit their output solely by radio (apart from some English language teaching programmes sold to foreign television services), it should be noted that 'radio', for BBC purposes and throughout this book, normally implies 'domestic radio', i.e. programmes intended to be heard within the United Kingdom. Similarly, 'the domestic services' means the output of the BBC's Radio and Television Directorates, excluding the External Services. The important point for the contributor to note is that there are thus three distinct markets, in television, in radio and in the External Services, of which the first two, for the non-professional writer, are much the more important. A second point to note is that members of the Board of Governors and Board of Management are not personally concerned in commissioning programmes. The decision whether or not to buy a particular contribution is made at a lower level and it is therefore pointless to address scripts to individual governors or Directors. Similarly, letters to the Chairman or Director-General complaining that a script has been unreasonably turned down are unlikely to increase a contributor's prospects of having his work accepted though they are always carefully investigated.

The Networks

While each of the four Managing Directors bears ultimate responsibility for his service's output, and for managing its resources efficiently, the key individuals who really determine the day-to-day pattern of broadcasting offered to the public are the Controllers in charge of the various networks. It is they who lay down the programme 'mix', i.e. the amount of different types of material broadcast, who draw up the schedules, which settle the placing and length of each programme, and who decide when to rearrange the advertised programme to accommodate a new or more topical item. The controllers have virtually no staff of their own, although, particularly in television, there is a large central planning staff concerned with the logistics of the television operation, which ensures, for instance, that the maximum use is made of every studio or film crew. The network controllers do not themselves have any responsibility for *making* programmes. Their job is to plan the most attractive and effective day or week, month or year, of programmes they can, drawing for the purpose on the various production departments (some of which, covering large areas of work, are organised into groups). The two sides, the programme makers and those who put their programmes on the air, are in constant informal contact, but the major decisions as to what programmes will be broadcast are taken at regular 'offers' meetings at which the heads of the various groups or

14

departments attend in turn and suggest lists of series, or individual programmes, they are prepared to make, together with an indication of their estimated cost. The controller, subject to the need to maintain a reasonable balance between different types of programme, and to provide for certain regular commitments such as the *Nine O'Clock News*, weighs up the attractiveness and the cost of the various offers made and then makes his choice among them. At the same time he may himself put forward ideas, or ask for suggestions to fill a particular place in the schedules, seeking, for example, a new comedy series for a particular evening, or inviting ideas for a late-night satire show for Saturdays. Except for certain special types of programmes, such as school broadcasts, all output departments – Drama, Light Entertainment, Current Affairs, etc. – make offers to both television networks and a proposal turned down by one controller may be accepted by the other, though each is aware of what the other has been offered. From the writer's point of view the important point is that programmes are suggested, and ultimately made, by the production departments, not by the networks. In other words, scripts and ideas should be sent to, say, drama department or religious broadcasting department, not to the Controller of BBC-1 or BBC-2.

The pattern in radio is similar, but not identical. Each of the four radio networks has its own Controller, but three of them, being overwhelmingly devoted to a specific type of music – 'pop' on Radio 1, light music on Radio 2 and classical music on Radio 3 – are much more closely linked to a particular supply department than is the case with television or with Radio 4. So far as spoken-word programmes are concerned, the Controllers of Radio 3 and Radio 4, like the Controllers of BBC-1 and BBC-2, 'buy' their programmes from common supply departments, with the exception of specialist talks on music commissioned by Radio 3. Drama Department (Radio), for example, produces plays for both Radio 3 and Radio 4 and Music Department supplies both with concerts. While, however, BBC-1 and BBC-2 both carry every type of programme, Radio 3 and Radio 4 are much more sharply distinguished in character. Radio 3 is very largely a serious music network, and carries only a small number of speech programmes and these exclusively of an intellectually demanding kind. Radio 4 is, on the other hand, basically a speech network, aimed at a more general audience and carrying only a few musical programmes, and little serious music. The same principle applies, however, to both. Programmes are actually commissioned and made by Drama, Talks and Current Affairs or some other production department to fulfil offers made to, or asked for, by the network controllers and it is with these production departments, not the controllers, that the outside contributor has to deal.

The Role of the Producer

It will be seen from the account given above that the idea for a programme or series may originate at various levels. It may come from the network controller, from the head of a group, from the head of a department, or, perhaps most commonly of all, from an individual producer, who may in turn have received it from an outside contributor. Ideas for subjects to be covered by established series like *Panorama* and *Everyman* almost invariably originate within the department concerned. It is the 'fictional' areas, such as light entertainment and drama, which offer the largest scope for the freelance and, in the case of radio, the large 'talks' field. Ideas which sound promising are occasionally made into pilot programmes, to enable the controller concerned to decide whether or not they are worth pursuing, and a successful 'one-off' programme may develop into a series. Besides looking out for and nurturing new ideas, a large part of the job of any head of department consists in providing the required number of episodes for an established series. Thus there are regular teams of producers working to fill the *Forty Minutes* documentary placing on BBC-2, or the *File on 4* current affairs spot on Radio 4. In a magazine-type programme several producers will be working simultaneously on different items, the idea in some cases having been put up by themselves, in others having been assigned to them. At any time, for example, several different producers will be preparing separate items for future editions of *Woman's Hour*, the format of which is already determined. Established series of this kind usually have an editor, whose function it is to supervise a number of producers, to take the major decisions on the subjects to be covered and to impose the final shape on each edition—a post not to be confused with that of 'script editor' or 'story editor'. In television, major series, or very important programmes, may have an Executive Producer, who is in overall charge, with one or more producers working to him who are directly responsible for various parts of the programme. Particularly in drama, but occasionally in other departments, too, it is not uncommon for there to be both a producer and a director working on a programme. In this case the producer normally controls the budgeting, casting, etc., and general shape of the programme, while the director is responsible for the filming on location and for directing the studio cameras.

In both radio and television the key person in commissioning and making a programme is the individual producer. It is usually the producer who chooses a subject or commissions a script, selects the actors or speakers to make the programme and handles the whole process of selling it on the air, from booking a studio to writing the billing for *Radio Times*. In the case of a new programme it is largely the enthusiasm and conviction which a producer puts into pressing his suggestion upon his head of department which decides whether the head of department supports it and presents it at his next 'offers' meeting, although, of course, either he or the network controller may nevertheless turn it down. Without support from a producer, however, a new idea stands little chance of acceptance, for the BBC's whole production system is founded upon giving a great deal of authority and independence to the individual producer. It is rare, though not unknown, for a producer to be instructed to make a programme about which he is unenthusiastic, and the budget allotted to a programme will to some extent depend upon the conviction with which a producer manages to convince his head of department of its potentialities and importance. Once it has been decided to make a programme, and the budget has been agreed, it is entirely the responsibility of the producer how his resources shall be allocated but he is expected to ensure that the final cost comes out very close to the permitted amount. The BBC is extremely cost-conscious. In television a system of total-costing is applied under which the producer is charged for all the facilities he uses, whether within the BBC, or from outside. In drawing up his programme budget he works from a standard rate-card which lays down exactly how much he will be charged for a day in the studio, for the use of a film crew, for the time given by the designer to designing his set, for the skilled man-hours required to make it, and so on. The cost of the script, even for a play, is likely to be one of the lesser items on the list, and the actual terms are not in fact negotiated by the producer but by the BBC's central Copyright Department, which provides a common service to all departments, in both Radio and Television, though the producer is consulted on the amount of the fee and may recommend a particular figure. The amounts involved in any television programme are very large, and it is therefore worthwhile for a writer to remember that a single extra scene, if it requires additional sets or extra time in the studio, or more outside filming, may add quite disproportionately to the production cost. The expense of television production to those unaware of the enormous complexity of the operation is often staggering. The cost of Light Entertainment productions averages £100,000 per hour, music, features and documentaries cost £80,000 per hour and drama £300,000. (There are, of course, wide variations between individual programmes and a major one-off series, like *Fortunes of War*, which will cost proportionately more than an episode of a regular serial like *EastEnders*.) The overall cost per hour of network television output is about £54,000. The overall cost of network radio per transmitted hour is about £5,400, but there are widespread variations between the four networks. Direct comparison with television is difficult, because in radio 'below the line' costs such as studio and similar facilities are not

17

included. The direct cost of radio drama, for example, is about £2000 per hour (with Radio 3 plays tending to cost rather more than those on Radio 4), although this figure rises to £6–7000 if costed in the same way as a television programme. Owing to radio's far smaller income, the producer will be working to a much tighter budget than his television counterpart and as the system of 'total costing' has not been introduced in radio his room for manoeuvre in allocating the programme allowance allotted to him will be very much less. The only items under his direct control, in the case of a play, for example, are the cost of the script, the cost of the cast and out-of-pocket expenses on 'travel and duty' ('T and D' in BBC jargon). From the writer's point of view the important distinction between the two media is that in the case of television the script is only one of many items with which the producer is concerned and the writer is only one of a whole army of specialists with whom he has to deal. In the case of radio the producer has far more limited technical and financial resources at his command but can, especially before the studio stage, concentrate on the script.

Once a script has been received, or unscripted material has been recorded, the producer is responsible for ensuring that nothing is broadcast which ought not to go on the air. Obvious hazards, to which he *will* be alert, and the script-writer *should be*, are incidental advertising (e.g. the unnecessary mention of brand names), libel, political bias, excessive violence, and – the most difficult area, since judgement here is necessarily largely subjective – bad taste. The BBC is often criticised both by those who complain that it is too permissive and by others who say it is too timid, and raise cries of 'Censorship!' whenever any gross obscenity or blatant piece of bias is deleted from a programme. Most regular viewers and listeners will be clear from the programmes which are broadcast what the reasonable limits of freedom of expression on the air are and the subject as a whole is outside the scope of this book. It should be noted, however, that the BBC, unlike Independent Broadcasting, is not subject to any statutory requirements in this area and that no machinery for exercising censorship over BBC programmes exists. The Governors of the BBC have, however, formally resolved that 'the Board accept that so far as possible the programmes for which they are responsible should not offend against good taste or decency or be likely to encourage or incite to crime or lead to disorder, or be offensive to public feeling'. To ensure that these aims are carried out the BBC relies upon a process of 're-ferring-up'. The producer is expected, as part of his normal responsibilities, to consult his head of department on any material which he is doubtful about including on grounds of taste and his immediate superior may, in turn, consult the Head of the Group. Thereafter, if necessary, the matter will be referred to the network Controller, to the Managing Director and even, in exceptional cases, perhaps where a whole programme is involved, to the Board of Management or even the Chairman of the Board of Governors.

Writing for Television

Some general comments

Certain obvious but often neglected points need to be borne in mind by all intending writers for television. First, since television is a visual medium scripts need to be conceived from the beginning in visual terms. Second, BBC-1 and BBC-2 are not comparable to the four radio channels, since each contains a complete range of programmes from light entertainment to serious Arts features. The character of the two networks does vary to some extent, as all regular viewers will recognise, since BBC-1 is designed to be the main, more popular network, which competes with ITV, while BBC-2, with a distinctive identity of its own, is designed to provide an alternative to BBC-1. The programmes on the two channels are thus intended to complement each other and to have as far as possible common programme junctions so that it is easy to switch from one channel to the other. Thus at the time of writing, when BBC-1 is carrying the classic serial *Vanity Fair* in the early evening on Sunday, BBC-2 is offering *Music in Camera*. At 8.00 p.m. on Thursday *Tomorrow's World*, on BBC-1, is set against *Call My Bluff* on BBC-2. Many, but by no means most, programmes which appear first on one channel are subsequently repeated on the other, and these 'cross-channel repeats' mean for the writer a substantially increased audience and, of course, the benefit of a repeat fee.

A third, general, comment, which the writer needs to bear in mind, is that television necessarily appeals to a mass market. Even a programme for a minority is likely to have a viewing figure far in excess of that of all but the most outstanding radio series. Scripts aimed only at a very limited audience will need to be of the highest standard if they are to stand a chance of acceptance.

Two of the medium's great assets are its intimacy and its mobility, which means that a story can move swiftly through space and time and that the writer can convey with few gestures and with spare, economical dialogue his dramatic intentions.

The BBC is always seeking new writing talent and has been instrumental in getting many new writers launched. It welcomes the submission of unsolicited scripts provided that the new writer is fully prepared for the great disappointment of rejection. To dull this disappointment it is worth stressing two things – that writing a play is far more difficult than most beginners realise, depending as it does not only on a craftsman's skills but also on a dramatist's instinct: and that the competition is extremely fierce. The information that follows may be helpful to those entering the television drama field for the first time; and perhaps even to established writers who are seeking new markets.

The Television Script Unit

BBC Television receives several thousand unsolicited scripts a year. The Script Unit provides a central point through which these scripts are channelled and is a means of bringing together the potential writer and the producer seeking new talent. It is probably of the greatest value to writers new to television, since established writers and literary agents often prefer to contact individual departments and, in the case of a Drama Group, script editors direct. The Unit provides guidance to outside contributors on where their work can best be placed, and information on the types of material being bought at a particular time. A leaflet, *Market Information for Writers*, revised as necessary, is available from Script Unit on request (please send a stamped addressed envelope). The unit also acts as a Script Information Centre for the benefit of producers, supplying them on request with the names of experienced writers who may be able to undertake particular commissions, and with details of any individual author about whom a producer may require information. All unsolicited scripts are read and assessed by one or more readers, and if an author shows promise he will be given encouragement by letter or by personal interview to develop his writing in the most practical direction. The successful writer with an established reputation in some other field, such as a novelist, is also given advice on the most likely field for his talents in television, while the full-time television writer seeking new work will be told which series are currently in need of contributions. The Unit does not itself commission work. This is done by individual departments, working, like radio, through the BBC Copyright Department, though in this case there is likely to be even closer and more constant contact between the writer and the producer than in the case of radio.

Enquiries should be addressed to the Head of Television Script Unit, BBC Television Centre, Wood Lane, London W12 7RJ.

Drama Group

By far the largest potential market for the outside contributor is the Television Drama Group, responsible for over 400 separate drama productions each year. The Group comprises five departments: in London, Plays Department and Series/Serials Department; in Birmingham, English Regions Drama; and in Glasgow and Cardiff the Scottish and Welsh Drama departments. Birmingham, Glasgow and Cardiff all produce plays, series and serials. A substantial part of Cardiff's output is in the Welsh language, for Sianel 4, to which both the BBC and ITV contribute programmes. While all of these are ready to receive suggestions and to meet new writers, there is general agreement that the best starting-point for the new writer is the individual or single-shot television play, which may either stand by itself or be part of a group of plays on some common theme. But this is not to say that Series and Serials are closed to the new writer; it is merely to underline that the competition in this area is of a particularly specialist kind. Scripts which are set outside London can be sent to the relevant Regional Drama Unit, or to the Script Unit, who will pass them on to the appropriate Region, providing the writing is of sufficient standard for further consideration.

Plays

An increasing number of one-off dramas are now being made on location on film. Plays Department therefore requires screenplays, with their greater emphasis on visual storytelling and atmosphere, as well as original studio dramas, where the emphasis is more on language and character. Whether intended for the studio or for film, scripts should be suitable for inclusion in one of the department's major strands – *Screen Two* or *Sunday Premiere*, which present a wide range of film dramas; The *Play on One*, which presents studio plays dealing with contemporary issues; or *Screenplay*, which mixes both studio plays and short films.

Required lengths are sixty, seventy-five or ninety minutes for television film scripts, and sixty or seventy-five minutes for studio dramas. There is no restriction as to subject matter, although historical dramas are more likely to meet objections on the grounds of expense. Perhaps the best rule for writers to follow is to write the sort of plays that they would like to see on the screen, choosing subjects from their own experience, or of which they have personal knowledge. Verse plays and adaptations of stage plays are generally not wanted. Before dramatising a novel or short story it is wise to check whether the BBC is likely to be interested. If the story is little known, a brief synopsis is helpful. The adapter should also make sure that the rights are available.

An established writer who submits the synopsis of a play may have the whole work commissioned on the strength of it. In the case of a new writer, synopses are of no value. In order to make a proper assessment, a completed script needs to be submitted.

Plays should be submitted, in the case of new writers, to the Script Unit. Those from writers already known to Drama Group can be sent direct either to one of the producers or Script Editors of the current single play series or to Head of Plays, Drama, Television, at the Television Centre.

Series and Serials

Series and Serials Department is a single unit within Drama Group, but as the two elements of its output are in some respects different they are described separately below.

22

Series

A series consists of a number of plays, each complete in itself, but with the same leading characters and a constant setting or theme. Series should deeply involve the characters and setting, so that a long run could, if necessary, be sustained, e.g. *One by One*. The Department is glad to receive, from individuals or from publishers, books which they feel might form the basis for a successful series.

Many writers for series are approached by the Department, who, after discussing a story-line, may commission a single episode for a series. Episodes are usually fifty-two minutes in length, though some are twenty-six minutes. The writer is normally given about three weeks to write a fifty-two-minute script, which is likely to be commissioned some three to five months ahead of production.

The department welcomes suggestions for new series. A synopsis should set out in some detail the aim and scope of the series. It should give details, too, of characters. A story-line for two or three episodes should be attached. The proposer of an idea which is accepted will probably not wish, or be able, to write all the episodes himself, but is normally given the opportunity to write at least some of them, receiving a small royalty in the case of the remainder. New contributors are expected to show proof of writing ability, and especially of good story-telling capacity. They may then be tried out on one episode of a series, usually one that is well established. Many contributors to series are novelists or former writers for radio. (Unpublished novels cannot be considered for serialisation.)

Serials

The term 'serial' covers two types of programme. One is the single story, which runs only for a set number of instalments, and is either adapted from a book (e.g. *Oliver Twist*) or specially written (e.g. *Dr Who*); the other is the running story which may continue for years (e.g. *Howard's Way*). The detailed requirements are dictated by the nature of the material. Normally the 'single story' adaptation runs from four to thirteen episodes, of thirty or fifty minutes, or, in the case of classics on BBC-2, for anything from two instalments, usually of fifty minutes, upwards. In long-running dramatisations, there is now some opportunity for new writers to be brought in, providing the writing is of sufficient standard. *EastEnders*, for example, has been a large user of new writers.

There is great competition for the writing of all types of television serials, particularly in the area of book or classic adaptation. These are much sought after by established writers and for the new writer to be approached for such work is rare. The author of a successful television play might be invited to contribute to a 'running story' serial, after being given the general story-line to be followed. New writers approached in this way may be expected to submit an episode 'on spec'. Although relatively lucrative, writing or contributing to a serial makes heavy demands on the writer, since the author of a 'single story' serial is expected to write all the instalments himself, which may be equal to writing five or six full-length plays, while a contributor to a 'running story' serial usually writes a substantial number of instalments, even though the story-lines are often supplied. There is, too, often considerable pressure to deliver scripts, since the department attempts in a long-running serial to keep several scripts ahead.

Potential contributors to either part of the Department's output should approach the Head of Series and Serials, Drama, Television, at Threshold House.

Light Entertainment Group

The Group is subdivided into two departments, one responsible for Comedy, the other for Variety.

Comedy

Comedy Department is concerned mainly with half-hour situation comedies (like *'Allo 'Allo*, *Ever Decreasing Circles* and *Yes, Prime Minister*).

Situation Comedies arise from one successful pilot episode. Further scripts are commissioned to make a series – usually six or seven episodes. These are written by the original authors and submissions for existing series are, therefore, not required. Every encouragement is given to new writers in this field, but as it is the most demanding type of writing, proven established professionals are, naturally, approached for new work. The laughs in a situation comedy should arise from interactions of characters and plot, not from a string of gags and funny lines. Scripts should have series potential – i.e., the same basic situation and characters can be used with many different story-lines. In general, it is a waste of effort to submit more than one pilot initially. Until this is accepted, or its basic concept at least, there is little future for further episodes. *Unless brilliantly original in treatment*, over-familiar themes (flat-sharing, football pool winners, etc.) are best avoided, as are subjects requiring too much outside location filming. The Light Entertainment Unit will supply a Guide Sheet which goes into this in more detail.

Although comedy can be judged only on treatment in a full script it is a good idea to send a very brief synopsis in the first instance in case the subject is, for some reason, unacceptable. Elaborate explanatory covering letters, detailed character histories and set descriptions are unnecessary; the script should speak

24

for itself. The Comedy Department employs Script Editors to assist writers in shaping their work for television but it is *not* their function to rewrite other people's work, nor are there writers on the staff to convert ideas into scripts. Neither can they undertake to arrange 'mating' with a collaborator, which is a personal matter.

Variety

Variety Department produces programmes which can vary in running time between twenty-five and fifty minutes. The output ranges across a wide spectrum and includes programmes based on a 'format', usually quiz shows (like *Call My Bluff* and *Bob's Full House*); shows built around a star singer (Val Doonican, Marti Caine) or shows built around a star comedian or entertainer (Les Dawson, Kenny Everett, Dave Allen, Des O'Connor). Variety Department also produces comedy revue, usually performed by a team (*Now – Something Else*), and shows containing elements of revue and situation comedy like *French and Saunders*.

All these shows variously demand either continuity material, questions, clues and puzzles and comedy material ranging in form and running time from a one-line gag, a 'quickie' lasting fifteen seconds or a minute, through to sketches which can run five minutes. There is a demand for both verbal and visual humour, and some comedy shows require specially written lyrics and parodies. However, opportunities to place unsolicited one-liners and sketches are usually only with revue-style programmes, such as *Russ Abbot* and *The Laughter Show*.

While material submitted will be read it is really only material that fits current needs that stands a chance of being used. It is, therefore, important to ring Light Entertainment Script Unit to enquire what shows are coming up. There is no call for comic songs and verse. Material is not passed on to comedians for use elsewhere, and audio cassettes are not required. There is rarely a market for quiz games, musicals, pantomimes, children's stories, personal reminiscences or manuscripts requiring adaptation.

All scripts and submissions whether for Comedy or Variety Department should be addressed to the Script Editor, Light Entertainment Group, at the Television Centre.

Current Affairs Department

The bulk of the Department's output consists of regular current affairs programmes, either the daily programmes, *Breakfast Time* and *Newsnight*, or the weeklies *Panorama, Question Time* and *The Money Programme*. Apart from its responsibility for mounting occasional programmes related to topical events, and for political coverage such as elections and the Party conferences, Current Affairs Department also produces occasional special film series. Generally speaking, Current Affairs output does not offer a market for the freelance writer, but there are occasions when a producer chooses to introduce freelance scripting effort for specialist knowledge or other reasons. The approach in such cases, however, comes from the producer, not the freelance writer.

Sports and Events Group

The Group is responsible for regular sports programmes such as *Grandstand* and *Sportsnight* which largely consist of a mixture of live and recorded material and new stories. It also produces all the major sporting events like the Olympic Games, World Cup, Commonwealth Games, together with coverage of other sport. The Group is also the producer of all State, Royal and Ceremonial occasions such as the Royal Wedding, Trooping the Colour, etc. The Group does not offer a market to the freelance writer.

Other Departments

The following Departments are not part of any of the Groups listed above and their respective heads work direct to the appropriate Network Controller.

Science and Features

The Department is primarily concerned with science programmes, ranging in content from pure scientific subjects to applied science and the social sciences. Its target audience ranges from people with a background of scientific understanding, and who are prepared to give sustained attention to a programme, to the average viewer with no special interest or knowledge. The Department originates several series. On BBC-1 *Tomorrow's World* is a half-hour studio and film magazine programme which deals in a popular way with technological advances. On BBC-2 *Horizon*, a weekly fifty-minute documentary film, deals in depth with a subject of current, but not necessarily of immediate, topical, interest. This series covers all aspects of science, medicine and technology; recent editions have included, *Can AIDS be stopped?*, *The Blind Watchmaker*, with Richard Dawkings, and *The John Wayne Syndrome* about stress-related problems amongst policemen.

On BBC-1 more general subjects are covered by the half-hour series, *QED*. The last series included, *Claws: A New Kind of Dinosaur*, and *Foolish Wise Ones* about idiot savants.

On both channels the Department produces special series. In recent years there have been James Burke's *The Day the Universe Changed*, and *Test Pilot* on BBC-1, and *Indelible Evidence* and *Edge of Life* on BBC-2. Occasionally the Department does dramas; among the most recent are *Threads* and *Life Story*.

As is often the case, it is difficult to separate the writing of documentary series from the conception and production of them. Serious consideration will always be given to any treatments, or scripts, sent in. If the idea is taken up every effort will be made to involve the contributor in the project concerned if he so wishes. If the contributor is an expert in a particular field, he might be asked to act as consultant or to develop and research the idea further. If he has experience in television he might be asked to join the production team in an appropriate capacity. The possibilities are varied, but in all cases due respect will be given to the authorship of any idea.

Treatments should take the form of a two- or three-page synopsis outlining the subject to be covered and the approach to it the writer is suggesting. This is quite sufficient initially, as at a later stage a more detailed treatment, including for instance names of likely contributors and the nature of major sequences, could be commissioned. If a contributor does have a project accepted and becomes involved in the production he will then need to be fully available for consultations.

Music and Arts

Programmes cover the whole range of the Arts, worldwide, including music and dance. Regular elements in this output are *Omnibus* (BBC-1) and *Arena* (BBC-2), a weekly programme covering aspects of the cinema, theatre, popular music and the visual arts. The Department also has a regular arts magazine programme, *Saturday Review*, and a monthly book programme, *Bookmark*. In general, contributors to programmes within these areas are approached by producers within the Department. However, anyone who feels he or she has an idea which would be of interest should write to the editor of the appropriate strand of output, sending not a full script but a succinct statement of the subject, the main points to be covered, and the manner in which it is proposed to treat the subject within the proposed programme or series. Where some particular event is concerned, *at least* six months' notice is generally required, and preferably longer.

Documentary Features

This Department makes relatively little use of submitted scripts but individual programmes or series of programmes do sometimes evolve from outlines or proposals sent in by outside writers. The Department makes a great many documentary films most of which originate from the producers and directors who make them and the scripts for these programmes are usually written by the film-makers. However, some freelance writers are

27

employed to write the commentary scripts, particularly when areas of special knowledge are called for. In these cases, and in all cases of collaboration between outside writers and programme producers, the writer must have shown the ability to work closely with the programme makers. The most likely way for a writer to turn a project into a programme is to submit an outline or treatment or programme idea and to develop this in co-operation with a particular producer or director.

The Department does make a limited number of dramatised documentaries, some of which begin with a proposal from a writer. It would be relatively rare for a fully-formed script to be the starting point of one of these productions. More likely, again, is that the proposal has been discussed and shaped with a programme maker before the commissioning of a script proper. Several magazine programmes also come from Documentary Features and the best way for any writer to submit items of short scripts for these is for them to do so direct to the editor or producer of the programme. Indeed, it is essential that anyone wishing to submit his or her writing should be aware of the style and format of the programmes to which he or she hopes to contribute. Correspondence should be addressed to Head of Documentary Features, Television, at Kensington House.

Children's Programmes

It is essential for any intending contributor to this Department's output to study the existing output before submitting material. Children's Programmes cover the entire spectrum of television from serious drama – plays, series and serials – and situation comedy to factual documentary programmes. For younger children *Play School* uses some unpublished stories and animated series are occasionally commissioned from outside scriptwriters. At present the upper age limit is thirteen and the Department is not looking for teenage material. Correspondence should be addressed to the Head of Children's Programmes, BBC Television Centre.

Presentation Department

The Department is responsible for creating the on-screen identity of both BBC-1 and BBC-2. Continuity is provided between programmes and includes introductions to programmes, announcements about programmes, mentions of associated products (i.e. books, records), and other programme information, as well as channel identification. Continuity Announcers write their own announcements. Presentation Department is also responsible for on-screen promotion or 'trailers' about forthcoming programmes. There is no market within this Department for unsolicited contributions.

Writing for Radio

The BBC Radio Directorate consists of the following programme departments: Drama; Light Entertainment; Features, Arts and Education; Radio 1, Radio 2 Music, Radio 3 Music, and Sport; and Outside Broadcasts. Radio News and Current Affairs is part of the BBC's general News and Current Affairs structure under the Deputy Director-General, who, as explained earlier, is also responsible for this part of the television output.

Of these departments, Radio 1 and Radio 2 Music, Radio 3 Music, and Sport and Outside Broadcasts do not require unsolicited material. There are separate radio departments for School Broadcasting and Religious Broadcasting. These will be dealt with later in this booklet as both Educational Broadcasting and Religious Broadcasting cover both radio and television and their respective heads are responsible for programme content in both media. Apart from News and Current Affairs, as indicated above, this does not apply to any other BBC programme department; and Drama Department (Radio), for example, can be considered from the writer's point of view as entirely separate from Drama Group (Television). The network controllers also draw on material produced in the three National and five English Regions outside London. The Head of Radio (whose title may vary slightly in different places) in each Region 'offers' programmes on the same basis as the radio production departments in London but covering the whole range of his radio output. The distinctive features of the various Regions are described under a separate heading later.

Drama Department

The Department is unlike others in radio in that, because its output is so large and varied, scripts are handled centrally, by the Drama Script Unit. The Unit consists of the Script Editor together with a number of editors and producers who specialise in different parts of the output. Any submitted script will therefore be considered for all possible outlets within the Department. For detailed guidance on current requirements and on the techniques of radio writing, the Script Unit issues a short pamphlet, *Notes on Radio Drama*, which will be sent on request.

In addition to plays, the output of the Department also includes a number of literary and feature programmes. It should be noted that the quality of a play is the decisive factor in its acceptance for broadcasting and that plays with a contemporary setting, historical plays, original plays and adaptations all receive equal consideration.

The regular requirements are as follows.

There is no specific requirement for subject matter or length, but material submitted must be complete plays which embody the highest standards of dramatic writing. While maintaining the tradition of excellence inherited from the Third Programme, Radio 3 Drama offers scope for new writing of distinction as well as representing classical drama.

Radio 4

This network now carries the greater part of the output of Drama Department, most of it in the form of regular weekly series. These vary not only in the length of the programme but also in character, the various placings requiring plays to some extent of a different kind. The difference is less in output than in the extent to which the treatment and language, and the nature of the plot, make demands upon the listener.

The Afternoon Play: This is a thrice-weekly spot of thirty to fifty-five minutes. It presents original radio plays on a wide variety of themes. *30, 45, 55, 60*

Saturday-Night Theatre: This is the longest established of all radio drama series, and requires ninety-minute narrative plays of an entertaining kind. It caters for a regular audience who prefer a popular 'good story' of the traditional kind to the more 'difficult' or experimental kind of drama. *90*

The Monday Play: This is normally broadcast for ninety minutes, and is the most demanding of the regular Radio 4 drama series. Adaptations of classical and modern works are sometimes placed here, but the major demand is for original plays. The essential feature of this series is that it assumes an audience interested in the play and ready to concentrate on it. *90, 105, 120, 75*

Serials: The regular drama serial is a weekly classic adaptation on Sunday afternoons in fifty-five-minute episodes. Original serials and adaptations of modern novels in thirty-minute episodes are also placed occasionally.

Citizens: launched in October 1987, is a long-running serial with an urban setting, in contrast to the rural background of *The Archers*. It is currently broadcast in two twenty-five-minute daytime instalments during the week, with a forty-five-minute omnibus edition on Saturday evening. The programme already has its own team of 'resident' writers and if this is extended it will be by invitation only.

Features of a wide variety of styles and content are considered for placing on both Radios 3 and 4.

Other programmes: The Department contributes also some individual speech programmes, and a number of anthology programmes, for occasional placing, where the subject-matter is drawn from drama and literature. It is, for instance, responsible for a number of poetry programmes on Radio 3 and Radio 4, but as the great majority of such programmes are produced by Documentary and Talks Department contributors are advised to submit material there in the first instance. (See under heading *Poetry* for details.)

Submission of Scripts

The Script Unit welcomes radio scripts from all sources, but in view of the very large number of these which are submitted every week, it cannot assess the potential for radio of scripts written for other media.

Where the writer has not already completed a script, he or she can submit a synopsis of the story with some pages of specimen dialogue in the first instance. This might avoid wasting time on an idea which may be unacceptable for reasons the writer is unlikely to be aware of, for example, that too many similar stories have recently been broadcast. Most plays, however, can only be judged from a completed script. For instance, a play consisting primarily of a study in depth of a particular relationship can probably only be assessed on the quality of the characterisation as revealed by the dialogue in full. New writers would therefore be unlikely to be commissioned to write such a play on the basis merely of a synopsis. On the other hand, a play depending for its effect on the ingenuity of its story-line can more easily be judged on a synopsis and some pages of specimen dialogue.

Scripts are acknowledged on receipt and, if rejected, are in due course returned, but owing to the number being handled at any one time a long delay in reaching a decision is often inevitable. A wait of two or three months, therefore, does not imply either that a play has been accepted or that it has been turned down – merely that it is being given thorough consideration. The governing factors are, first, the number of scripts already awaiting consideration and, second, the extent to which the author has already considered the radio potential of his work and indicated this in the submitted material. The more information the author gives about his intentions, the easier it is to assess the possibilities of an idea.

The Unit also exists to advise and encourage emergent talents, for which reason authors are often invited to discussions at Broadcasting House in London or at BBC headquarters in the provinces. It is clearly impossible, however, for the staff to meet every would-be author, so that such a meeting is only proposed after a specific script or project has been submitted and considered.

Some General Points

Radio Drama provides a large and relatively stable market for the author and one which has a constant demand for a wide variety of material. The nature of the medium, too, is such that the author's contribution to a final production is very much greater than in, say, television or on the stage. For these reasons writers have in the past found radio a particularly satisfying medium and the Department is eager, as a matter of policy, to add each year to the list of successful radio dramatists.

The immediate rewards for radio writing are less than those for television but there are considerable opportunities for the exploitation of a radio play. Within the BBC alone, there is the possibility of repeats on the domestic services, broadcasts on the External Services, and sales by the Transcription Service, all of which attract further payment. In addition, there is an international market in radio drama, and as the BBC is the world's leading source of such drama, this can also bring in substantial additional fees.

All scripts should be addressed to: Script Editor, Drama (Radio), BBC, Broadcasting House, London W1A 1AA. A stamped addressed envelope should be enclosed if the sender wishes unwanted material to be returned.

Light Entertainment Radio

This is a rather specialised market, which leans heavily on experienced writers with proven success. However, all manuscripts submitted are carefully considered and may be used. Scripted output falls into two main categories:

The situation comedy, comprising a plot built round a set of characters which, though funny enough to make a studio audience laugh, possesses some degree of credibility. Such programmes are half an hour long. Examples are *The Random Jottings of Hinge and Bracket* and, for those recorded without a studio audience, *King Street Junior* and *After Henry*.

The 'anything goes' type of show, which is simply designed for laughter and makes no attempt to tell a story, although it may follow a theme. This comprises separate sketches, and is performed by a team, e.g. *The Good Humour Guide*, *Radio Active*, or can be a vehicle for a particular performer, e.g. Ernie Wise in *Wise on the Wireless*. There are also occasional 'act' shows, headed by a star comedian, such as *The Frankie Howerd Show* and *Dawson and Castle*.

These categories are listed only to show the *kinds* of programme Light Entertainment does. Speculative half-hour scripts for actual shows already on the air are a waste of everybody's time, as known writers will already have been contracted to do each entire series. New writers interested in the thirty-minute market must submit new projects.

Effective judgement can be made only on receipt of a complete script: but comment and advice can be offered on the basis of a detailed synopsis with pages of sample dialogue. Where the material is designed for a particular comedian, it may save the writer's time to contact the latter first – possibly by sending him material for his act – since he may write his own material or not be available for radio work.

There is a third category of radio Light Entertainment, which may be the most fruitful means of approach for new speculative writers. This is the sketch show, usually topical, for which sketches are accepted from any source if they are funny enough and meet the producer's needs. Prime examples of this genre are *Week Ending* (Friday night satire, repeated on Saturday, on Radio 4) and *The News Huddlines*, the Radio 2 topical satire show. There are sometimes other such sketch shows open to general contributors, which the listener can usually identify from the long list of writers' credits at the end. Contributions should be sent direct to the producer of the show in question.

How to Submit Material

Thirty-minute comedy manuscripts to: The Script Editor, Light Entertainment (Radio), BBC, Broadcasting House, London W1A 1AA.

Sketches for individual comedy shows to: the producer concerned (see *Radio Times*) at the above address.

Features, Arts and Education

This Department is responsible for a wide range of speech programmes, including the arts, science and magazine programmes for Radio 4 and Radio 3. Features, Arts and Education combines the departments formerly responsible for Talks and Documentaries, Archive Features and Continuing Education. The Continuing Education output, however, remains the responsibility of the Controller, Educational Broadcasting; and its requirements, so far as the writer is concerned, are therefore indicated later in this booklet in the section dealing with Educational Broadcasting.

The Arts

The Department's main coverage of the arts on Radio 4 is in the programme *Kaleidoscope*. The contributors to the programme are mainly authors, artists, directors and critics. They are invited by the producers. Information and ideas should be addressed to the Editor, *Kaleidoscope*, Talks and Documentaries, Radio, Broadcasting House, London W1A 1AA.

Poetry

In addition to anthologies and critical programmes which feature or discuss published poetry, both classical and contemporary, there are two series, both on Radio 3, which are devoted to recent work. *The Living Poet*, an occasional series, is confined to the work of one poet selected on the initiative of the producer. *Poetry Now*, broadcast once a month at a duration of twenty minutes, is made up of readings of unpublished verse. Material for this programme should be sent to the Editor, *Poetry Now*, Broadcasting House, London. Radio 4 broadcasts regular poetry series, but these offer no outlet for unpublished work by living writers.

Science

Scripted talks are usually most acceptable at twenty minutes' duration and should be by scientists who are prepared to broadcast their own scripts. Ideas for science documentaries and features are best submitted initially in a brief outline. Ideas and recorded material for the weekly Radio 4 magazine, *Science Now*, and for *Medicine Now*, are also of interest. Correspondence should be addressed to Chief Producer, Science Programmes, Talks and Documentaries Radio, Broadcasting House.

Documentaries and Features

Documentary programmes consist mainly of original interviews and recordings. Their subjects are as varied as life itself. Most documentaries are commissioned by staff.

Features, that is programmes based mainly on the printed word, are accepted from outside contributors. The initial idea should be submitted in a brief outline and, if it is acceptable, the writer may be asked to expand this into a full synopsis and to write two or three pages of the proposed script including extracts from the sources and the proposed narration. Ideas and proposals should be sent to The Head of Talks and Documentaries, Broadcasting House.

News and Current Affairs

Radio News and Current Affairs is responsible for a large output. It includes *Newsbeat* on Radio 1, and the 'sequences' of news and current affairs programmes on Radio 4. The main programmes are *Today*, produced by Morning Current Affairs, *The World at One, PM*, and *The World This Weekend*, produced by Afternoon Current Affairs, *The World Tonight*, produced by Evening and Special Current Affairs, and *The Financial World Tonight*, produced by the Financial Unit. The editors work directly to Editor, News and Current Affairs. They commission all the material they need and do not require unsolicited scripts. *PM* makes daily use of listeners' letters but these are read professionally in the studio and are not paid for.

Evening and Special Current Affairs also produces *The Week*

in Westminster, From Our Own Correspondent and *Inside*
ment, as well as special programmes. It does not use unso
work from outside contributors.

Magazine Programmes

Magazine Programmes Department has a large output of about
fifteen regular weekly or daily programmes, and an ad hoc series
of talks or features from its Features Unit. The main opportunities for short scripts are in *Morning Story* (see later); *Woman's
Hour* and *You and Yours* rarely use short scripted talks nowa-
days. *You and Yours, Woman's Hour* and *Feedback* do make use
of listeners' letters, but for these no payment is made. Neither is
payment made for listeners who contribute to phone-in programmes such as *Call Nick Ross*.

Another responsibility of Magazine Programmes is *In Touch*,
a fifteen-minute weekly programme for visually handicapped
people. Most of the contributors are themselves blind or partially
sighted and the producer is always pleased to receive short scripts
concerning interesting personal experiences or making points of
general importance. There are similar requirements for *Does He
Take Sugar?*, a weekly thirty-minute programme about people
suffering from other types of disability. The Department's Features Unit occasionally produces a variety of scripted talks:
usually ten or fifteen minutes long and often in series of three to
six. Complete scripts should not be sent in the first instance, but
would-be contributors should submit a treatment of their idea,
and how it would be developed in each talk.

In many ways the Department's best outlet for either the
amateur or professional writer is *Morning Story*, a daily short
story of fifteen minutes' duration. This programme is radio's
main outlet for original short story writing and its policy is to use
only a small proportion of previously published work. Stories
should be of about 2500 words. There is a preference for a strong
plot rather than impressionistic writing.   *2100 — 2300.*

The essential point which needs to be remembered both in
writing short stories and also short radio talks is that scripts
should be written for reading aloud and thus have a simple and
direct construction without long literary sub clauses or strings of
adjectives. Short stories in particular can give scope to an actor to
'perform'. The best talks are often those where the writer is
burning to communicate some idea or to recount some experience. Indignation, if properly controlled, is often an effective
source of inspiration. Speakers with local accents are welcome
both in programmes made in London and in those produced in
the network production centres. In the case of short scripts the
writer will normally be invited to broadcast the script himself,
but with longer broadcasts as in the *Morning Story* slot it is usual

that a professional actor or presenter be engaged to read the script. Occasionally, authors read their own stories, but this is the exception and is confined to those with experience of broadcasting.

Would-be contributors to *Morning Story* should send their scripts direct to the 'Morning Story Office' at Broadcasting House. All other contributions should be sent to the producers of the respective programmes mentioned or, in the case of uncertainty, to the Head of Magazine Programmes, Radio.

Woman's Hour is also part of Current Affairs Magazine Programmes. Listeners' letters are always most welcome for the programme's correspondence column and the editor is always glad to hear of listeners' personal experiences which might make the basis for a feature or interview. Scripts, however, are no longer used. The address for all letters is: *Woman's Hour*, Broadcasting House, London.

Some editions are produced outside London in the four English regions and by BBC Wales, Scotland and BBC Northern Ireland. Ideas and suggestions intended for them should be submitted to the appropriate headquarters.

Educational Broadcasting

The BBC's output in the field of educational broadcasting is under the direction of a single Controller, and is planned as a whole. For the purposes of the outside contributor, however, it is best considered in four departments, School Broadcasting, Television, and School Broadcasting, Radio; and Continuing Education, Television, and Continuing Education, Radio. In addition the BBC, through the Open University Productions Unit, works in partnership with the Open University in providing the broadcasting element in the University's courses.

School Broadcasting

The BBC's output caters for children of around four years to pupils of school leaving age and beyond. The programmes aim to provide material that is informative, stimulating and entertaining and which makes good use of the broadcasting medium. Some series aim to make a contribution to a planned course of study but others, such as *A Service for Schools*, are intended for general stimulus and enrichment. The aims of all series of school programmes for radio or television are laid down by the School Broadcasting Council, which consists largely of representatives of members of the teaching profession.

The main difference between school broadcasting and general broadcasting is that school series are planned, sometimes in detail, at least eighteen months before transmission and that the audience for any particular series is clearly defined by age and sometimes by ability. Consequently a writer would need to be involved in programmes well in advance and would also need to have a knowledge of and a sympathy for a particular age or ability range of young people.

Some series for schools are produced by, and broadcast only in, Scotland, Wales and Northern Ireland. Enquiries should be addressed to one of the following at the appropriate headquarters: Head of Educational Broadcasting, Scotland (located at Edinburgh); Head of Educational Broadcasting, Wales (at Cardiff); Producer (School Broadcasting) Northern Ireland (at Belfast).

School radio and television are equal in status to all other departments of the BBC. They are not a training ground from which writers can graduate to writing for adults; moreover writers may have the additional discipline of writing to a close brief, of simplifying complicated ideas and arguments and of using a suitable vocabulary for a child audience. Teaching experience is not essential, but often useful.

Only a minority of school broadcasts are directly instructional. They aim to help teachers, by providing them with an additional resource that makes full use of the medium, not to replace them. Writers should watch or listen to as many school programmes as possible and study the BBC's *Annual Programmes*, available each year from April onwards. These list all broadcasts for the coming academic year and can be obtained free of charge from: the Secretary, Educational Broadcasting Council, Villiers House, The Broadway, Ealing, London W5 2PA.

Television

Most school television programmes are written by the producer or an academic specialist working in conjunction with the producer. Such specialists are usually known to the producer in advance and approached by him. Some series transmit information in dramatised form. The careers series *Going to Work*, for example, may reveal through acted scenes the problems of starting work and relationships with older colleagues. Here non-specialist writers experienced in drama are used. The writer needs to work to a close brief, to understand young people and their working life and work to the exigencies of a television budget. Yet the writing still needs to be of good quality that the audience will recognise as stimulating and as an accurate reflection of life. These plays are twenty minutes long. Series for younger children also often use storytelling in this way for taking a view of the outside world or recreating the past.

The series *Scene* also contains specially written plays for teenagers; these plays have a wide brief. Most of the writing for this series has been by established writers well known to adult viewers. But exciting, amusing, stimulating writing would always be considered, whoever the writer. These plays are twenty-eight minutes long.

The opportunities for writers to contribute to the work of the Department are limited compared with the quantity of the Department's output, but writers who feel they have a contribution to make should send scripts or outline treatments to the Head of School Broadcasting (Television), at Villiers House, The Broadway, Ealing, London W5 2PA.

Radio

The Department can only offer limited scope to new writers. They should submit a brief note of their background or qualifications and some examples of their writing. These need not have been intended for radio but it is helpful if they include some dialogue. The Department broadcasts a certain amount of poetry, often previously unpublished, but except for *Listening Corner*, all programmes are made for listeners in schools and colleges. At present the Department does not produce regular entertainment programmes for children to listen to at home. Some expansion in this area is planned for the future but no date for this development has yet been fixed. Contributors are expected to show an awareness of the current radio output for schools and evidence of some familiarity with the series for which they hope to work. The qualities looked for in scripts are originality and a lively form of presentation, and a writer must be able to accept constant guidance from the producer and write to a tight brief. High academic qualifications are not essential since the Department has access to consultants who may provide guidance on script content. However, an ability to research a topic is often called for. Programmes may be ten, fifteen or twenty minutes in length. In all series a modern idiom in the writing, and an awareness of the contemporary world, are looked for and the Department is particularly interested in writers who are seeking to develop new forms and techniques in radio and to apply them in the interest of young listeners. There is also scope for contributors who can conduct interviews and write linking material for documentary programmes. Experience in using a portable recorder and editing tape is a considerable advantage for this type of programme.

Foreign Languages: Contributors can be commissioned, both to write programmes, some of which include an element of direct teaching, and to introduce programmes. The main requirement is for writers who speak French and German as their native language, and are able to employ a limited vocabulary, but there are opportunities from time to time in Spanish, Russian and Italian.

History: The majority of history scripts are fully dramatised or take the form of dramatised documentaries. Programmes sometimes include actuality that has been recorded and edited by the contributors themselves. Potential contributors are strongly advised to acquaint themselves with the style, content and level of difficulty of the various history series.

Religion: School Broadcasting, not Religious Broadcasting, is responsible for all religious broadcasts to schools, and there is a constant demand for suitable material. Whilst it is valuable for writers to be familiar with the current principles influencing Religious and Moral Education above all the requirement is for sensitive writers of high calibre, particularly those with an interest in biography and P.S.E. (Personal and Social Education).

Potential contributors to all school radio series should submit details of their qualifications and experience, and a note of the series to which they would like to contribute, to the Head of School Broadcasting (Radio), 1 Portland Place, London W1A 1AA.

Continuing Education

BBC Continuing Education programmes are planned on an annual basis in consultation with the Educational Broadcasting Council. The content of the various series is settled from several months to a year or more ahead. Similarly supporting publications are usually prepared well in advance of transmission. Details of all series are printed in periodic *Learning at Home* supplements in *Radio Times*.

Television

The Department from time to time commissions scripts or treatments and supporting pamphlets from outside writers who are authorities or experts on the subject. Only very occasionally can unsolicited scripts be accepted though ideas for new series, for broadcasting in some future year, will be considered. Suggestions should take the form of a statement of the proposed series, a synopsis of the content of each programme, and perhaps a detailed treatment of one programme. The normal programme length is twenty-five minutes, and series normally consist of between five and ten programmes. Very few programmes have any drama content.

The areas of output include science and information technology, work and management, social affairs, foreign languages, literacy and numeracy, health and consumer education.

Correspondence should be addressed to the Head of Continuing Education, BBC Television, Villiers House, The Broadway, London W5 2PA.

Radio

Some Continuing Education programmes are now placed on Network Radio 4 on a quarterly basis. Others are broadcast on Radio 4 FM on Saturday and Sunday afternoons. There is virtually no opportunity to accommodate unsolicited scripts. However, Head of Continuing Education, Radio, welcomes suggestions for future programmes – normally developed in series form – from writers who feel they have a contribution to make. Intending contributors should be familiar with styles used on Radio 4 and should make a point of listening to *Options* on Saturdays and Sundays (4.00–6.00 p.m. FM).

The Open University

The Open University, launched in January 1971, enables students in full-time employment to work for degrees in their spare time, through correspondence tuition, study at home, and radio and television programmes. The programmes are part of a series of highly integrated courses prepared by University academic staff and BBC producers working closely together, and though outside contributors are often used in broadcasts, they are normally other university teachers or similarly qualified specialists. The BBC's Open University Production Centre therefore offers few openings for the freelance or part-time writer, and in particular it is pointless to submit a complete script since it is most unlikely to be accepted. However, writers who have a particular interest, and qualifications, in one of the topics in a specific course can, if they wish, submit a brief outline for an appropriate television or radio programme to the Head of Programmes, BBC O.U.P.C., Walton Hall, Milton Keynes MK7 6BH. Those wanting to know more about future courses should write for the University guide for applicants, which can be obtained free on application to: The Admissions Office, The Open University, P.O. Box 48, Walton Hall, Milton Keynes MK7 6AA.

Religious Broadcasting

The Religious Broadcasting Department is responsible for all regular religious broadcasting in television and radio. It makes a wide range of programmes for both television channels and all four domestic radio services. The broad aim of its work is to reflect the religious life of the country and though the mainstream of Christian orthodoxy predominates there are growing opportunities for expression outside it, including representation of Christian minority groups, other religions, and non-religious systems of belief. (Programmes on such subjects may also be broadcast by Talks and Documentaries Department (Radio) or the comparable departments in television.)

Television

Little use is made of unsolicited material, but some opportunities for the new writer do exist. Various programmes also require material for dramatised documentaries. These range from historical scripts on religious themes to dramatisations of contemporary situations – for example, Christians on trial for their faith. The remarks made under the 'Radio' heading below in respect of sermons and broadcast services apply equally to television.

Material should be addressed to the Head of Religious Broadcasting at Television Centre.

Radio

Unsolicited scripts, or ideas or synopses of talks, are welcome for *Pause for Thought* on Radio 2 (live, duration two and a half minutes), and on Radio 4 for *Thought for the Day* (live, three and a half minutes), *Prayer for the Day* (recorded, four minutes) and *Seeds of Faith* (recorded, fourteen minutes). *Prayer for the Day* is devotional in style and usually ends with a prayer; *Thought for the Day* should reflect what people *do* as a result of what they believe. *Pause for Thought* is popular in style and personal in content. *Seeds of Faith* explores contemporary spirituality. The Department is also willing to hear from academically or professionally qualified individuals whose recent work and thinking, whether in published form or not, might fairly be supposed to interest the general listener to Radio 3. Submissions can be in the form of scripted talks of about twenty minutes in length, or of a synopsis. They should be addressed to the Religious Broadcasting Department. Suggestions for single documentaries are welcome as are suggestions for possible broadcasters.

The Religious Broadcasting Department always welcomes news from religious communities for its news and current affairs programme *Sunday*. In addition it is helpful to know of churches from which an effective Outside Broadcast might be mounted.

Correspondence should be directed, in the first instance, to the Head of Religious Programmes (Radio) at Broadcasting House, London.

The English Regions

The five English Regions contribute to the BBC's output in three ways. First, on the television side, they provide a platform in which regional affairs can be discussed by people of the Region for the Region in the context of their nightly news magazines, which run from 6.00 to 6.25 p.m. on weekdays, while the Regions opt-out of BBC-1. A number of feature programmes are also produced by each Region, intended to provide material of specific interest to the regional audience, and placed in opt-out slots from BBC-2. The nature of these programmes varies from Region to Region and often from week to week, but all enable the regional Heads of Television to develop the ideas and talents of their own production staff and of regional contributors and artists. Some of these programmes may later be repeated on the national networks.

Second, each Region already contributes, or will contribute, both radio and television programmes to the national networks. These cover between them the full variety of programme areas but individual Regions have developed their own areas of specialisation and most of the programmes of that particular type will therefore be made by them. Each Region is therefore in effect a network production centre, whose staff are of the same professional calibre as those working in comparable departments in London and who expect to draw on the same range of writers and performers.

Third, each Region contains a number of local radio stations. Their staff play an important role as part of the BBC's news-gathering network, but their main task is to provide a distinctively local service within their catchment area.

Local Radio

The first BBC Local Radio stations went on the air in 1967. There are now thirty-two in operation in England and the Channel Islands. Some have additional 'satellite' stations which opt-out at certain times in the day. A further eight stations are planned to complete the chain by 1990.

As the output of each station varies, any intending contributor should listen to his own station and study the schedules of its programmes in *Radio Times*. Contributions from people not living or working within the reception area of a station are not normally considered. Despite the differences in their output, all the local stations have certain characteristics in common. Each originates a proportion of its own output which ranges from twelve hours or more for the larger stations to around six for the smaller. For the rest of the day it transmits one of the national networks, usually Radio 2. All operate on both FM and medium wave, and serve a distinct and clearly defined local community: a city and its immediate rural environs, a county, a conurbation, or, in the case of Radio London, the whole of Greater London. Every station aims to provide a service of local news and a forum for the discussion of local issues, and to help develop participation by members of the community in local affairs and activities of all kinds. The small staff of twenty-five to thirty work under such pressure that they have little opportunity to consider long and elaborate scripts; and the whole atmosphere of local radio is one of much more direct and informal contact between broadcaster and listening public than is possible at the national level. The station manager has a great deal of autonomy, and is entirely responsible for his own programme schedules. The basic equipment for all stations consists of two self-operated cubicles with an adjoining studio, while the larger stations also have an additional studio. Funds are very limited and the fee paid to most contributors nominal, except, for example, for professional journalists contributing to news programmes, whose work is covered by a national agreement. The manager can, however, draw on the national resources of the BBC, for example, for a news service, and is advised by a Local Radio Council of residents interested in local radio and in touch with various aspects of the life of the community. All the stations try to be genuinely local in inspiration and to tailor their output to the special needs and interests of their listeners, who may, for example, include a high proportion of retired people, or industrial workers, or ethnic minorities. All have a far more flexible approach to programme planning than is possible on the national networks, so that programmes are sometimes allowed to overrun, discussions may be 'open-ended' or the whole published schedule may be re-arranged to accommodate some unforeseen event. The peak listening times for most stations are in the early morning from about 7.00 to 9.00 a.m., in mid-morning, and in the early evening around 4.30 to 7.00 p.m. The weekends usually provide a space for religious programmes, arts magazines and discussion programmes of interest to the whole family, together with entertainment programmes for young people and of course sport. All the stations work closely with local organisations, so that, for example, literary material may be submitted via a local Writer's Circle, a religious programme may be planned by a group of local clergy, youth groups may join together to produce a teenage magazine programme.

An important part of the output of all stations is educational, both formal and informal. These programmes are normally produced as joint ventures between the local station and various outside educational bodies. A large number of teachers are directly involved in their production, frequently through their local teachers' centres. Anyone wishing to take part in such programmes should consult the Education Producer at the local radio station.

Each station has a character of its own but in all of them the prevailing mood is that of the informality referred to earlier. Usually about two-thirds of the locally originated material is based on the spoken word, and informality means that many programmes rely upon unscripted interviews and discussion. Apart from the news bulletins, formal in character and prepared by the professional news staff, the station will be seeking contributions from the community to topical programmes, some intended for the whole audience, others for particular groups such as women or young people. The output is also likely to include religious programmes, programmes for specialist groups, gardeners, motorists and fishermen, for example, the education programmes already mentioned and programmes on the local arts.

Given a good idea, all stations offer the opportunity for someone interested in radio to learn more about broadcasting, to take part in a programme, and perhaps to be involved in its planning and presentation. The local stations are always willing to consider ideas set out in a few sentences, either for items in existing sequences or for new programmes, and also short scripts, normally of three to four minutes, say 4–500 words, quite often read at the microphone by the author. Longer scripts, of up to fifteen minutes, will be considered, but if a whole series is proposed only the first script should be sent. Suggestions for subjects which might be covered in programmes, not necessarily involving the contributor himself, are also welcome. For magazine programmes a relatively light-hearted approach is welcome, though not essential. Poems of perhaps twenty to thirty lines can be offered to stations broadcasting an Arts programme, as can short stories, on any subject, up to fifteen minutes long. Where a contribution is intended for a specific programme it should be addressed to the producer concerned. In other cases material can be sent to the Manager, at one of the addresses given later.

BBC Midlands

BBC Midlands covers a very large area, stretching from the Welsh border in the west to Lincolnshire in the east, from the Forest of Dean to the Derbyshire peaks, with a population of eight million people. Its principal production centre is at Pebble Mill in Birmingham, one of the three main broadcasting centres in England outside London, and the first regional purpose-built broadcasting complex. Each year more than 500 hours of television for the network and around 2000 hours of network radio are produced there. Pebble Mill also makes programmes for the

Region itself, and includes the local radio station, BBC Radio WM. There are also television studios at Nottingham in the East Midlands and seven local radio stations, BBC Radio Derby, Leicester, Lincoln, Nottingham, Shropshire, Stoke and, already mentioned, WM, serving the Birmingham area. Two more local radio stations are in the planning stage, to serve respectively Warwickshire, and Hereford and Worcester.

The Head of Broadcasting at Pebble Mill is responsible for both radio and television output and works closely with the Heads of Network Radio and Television. They periodically visit London to attend 'offers' meetings where they 'sell' programmes to the London-based Controllers. There is also direct contact between production staff at Pebble Mill and their related departments in London.

Network Television

Pebble Mill, with its three television studios, has established a high reputation for drama, light entertainment and daytime television, which it pioneered. Drama series such as *Lizzie's Pictures*, and *Heart of the Country* were produced in the large Studio A and on location. Other well-known series made in Birmingham include *Howard's Way*, and *Vanity Fair*.

The Head of Drama, Television, has responsibility for contributions to such series as *Screen 2* and other single plays produced and directed at Pebble Mill. He will seek out creative talent in his field from the whole of England. Ideas for plays, series or serials which have not been submitted to London for consideration can be sent to the drama script editor's department for consideration, preferably in the form of several pages of dialogue and a synopsis of the rest of the script.

Pebble Mill's history of daytime television is a long one. As long ago as 1972 it introduced *Pebble Mill at One* from the building's foyer which doubles as a studio. The recent upsurge of daytime television throughout the BBC has been led by Pebble Mill programmes such as *The Clothes Show* and *Daytime Live*, both of which have proved very popular. Special interest programmes have also flourished at Pebble Mill, though *Top Gear, Gardeners' World, Ebony, On the House*, all network agricultural output, programmes for the Asian community and other specialist strands offer openings only for the most experienced contributor. The same is true of light entertainment programmes such as *Telly Addicts, The Golden Oldie Picture Show, Phil Cool* and major televised pop concerts.

Correspondence about all programmes other than drama should be sent to the Head of Network Television at Pebble Mill.

There are five radio studios at Pebble Mill from which come a wide range of documentary, drama, music and magazine programmes for the four BBC Radio networks.

Pebble Mill, for instance, produces a minimum of ten editions a year of Radio 4's *Woman's Hour*, but it is also in constant contact with Current Affairs Magazine Programmes in London over the provision of individual items for the 'London' edition. Other Current Affairs Magazine Programmes such as *You and Yours* and *Does He Take Sugar?* are provided with two or three items a week from Pebble Mill. Submissions for *Woman's Hour* should be sent to the Producer, *Woman's Hour*, Pebble Mill.

One producer at Pebble Mill is responsible for the Midlands contribution to the *Morning Story* series on Radio 4. On average, one of these stories is transmitted every three weeks. Original and preferably unpublished material of around 2400 words should be submitted to the Producer, *Morning Story*. Stories should be written specifically for the spoken word and contemporary themes are preferred.

Radio documentaries and features of from thirty to sixty minutes are also produced at Pebble Mill, the general nature of the requirements being the same as for those made in London. Ideas in the form of a short synopsis should be addressed to the Senior Producer, Features Documentary (Radio), Pebble Mill.

An important part of Pebble Mill's output, in radio as in television, is drama. The Birmingham drama producers contribute to all the major Radio 4 and, on occasion, Radio 3 drama series. They receive a large number of unsolicited scripts each year, but welcome more, and all plays offered are read by the producer. A Birmingham producer may reject a script but, if he likes it, send it to the Drama Department in London for a further opinion. If accepted, the script will then be commissioned from Birmingham and will almost certainly be produced there. Drama producers in the Midlands, like their counterparts in London, regularly invite promising authors to meet them to discuss their work and, on occasion, take the initiative in commissioning work from writers already known to them.

It is not essential for all plays offered to Birmingham to be set in the Midlands. Generally, there is no advantage in a writer based outside the region submitting a play to Birmingham rather than to London; though there are cases where the piece may have a Midland setting and therefore be more immediately accessible to a producer who knows the area. Provided such a play has not already been rejected by London and the author clearly states his or her reasons for submitting it to Birmingham, the script will be read. Suggestions for dramatisations of novels and other prose works are generally accepted only from established writers. Suggestions for dramatised feature programmes are particularly welcome.

One of the most celebrated – and certainly the longest-running – programmes to come from Midlands radio is *The Archers*, first heard as a daily serial in 1951. It has been the recipient of the Sony Gold Award for services to radio. Unsolicited suggestions for *The Archers* are unlikely to be considered.

Music programmes obviously offer little scope for outside offerings, though ideas for such programmes should be sent to the Head of Network Radio.

In general, BBC Midlands is pleased to welcome programme ideas, suggestions, scripts and other such contributions from both new and established writers, whether for radio or television, network or regional. The best chance of success for such contributions lies in their being sent to the correct person or department for assessment, as indicated above.

Regional Television

BBC Midlands Television has studios in Birmingham and Nottingham, plus the use of local radio newsrooms and facilities for Outside Broadcasts. As well as the morning 'opt-out' news bulletins from East and West Midlands, Regional Television also produces the nightly magazine programme *Midlands Today* plus feature programmes of special interest to the area such as *Crimewatch Midlands, Life File* and *Frontline*.

Suggestions for news coverage should go to the Head of News and Current Affairs and for other fields to the producer of the programme in question.

Radio Derby

BBC Radio Derby went on the air officially in April 1971, but it had been given permission to broadcast special programmes in February of that year, following the totally unexpected collapse of Rolls-Royce, Derby's largest employer. A makeshift studio was constructed at the Sutton Coldfield transmitter site and those early programmes, broadcast at a critical time for the local community, did much to win the station a special place in the hearts of its listeners.

Now, from its studio premises near the city centre, Radio Derby broadcasts for about ninety hours a week to the three-quarters of a million people who live in mid and South Derbyshire and East Staffordshire. The area is predominantly rural with less than half of the population living in the conurbations of Derby and Burton-on-Trent, the rest being scattered in small market towns, villages and remote communities. Highly sophisticated technology at the British Rail Research Centre and the massive Rolls-Royce aero engine complex contrast with the skills of the sheep farmers in the Peak District.

The station tries to reflect the diversity of Derbyshire and East Staffordshire with programmes about specific people and areas of interest, e.g. *Aaj-kal* (news, views and music from the local Asian community); *Black Roots* (from the Afro-Caribbean community); *Sunday Sound* ('A look at the world through the eyes of faith'); *The Arts Show* (about people making the news in the Arts), and *Farm & Country* (for all those interested in the countryside). There are evening programmes for lovers of country music, jazz, folk, nostalgic melodies, gospel, soul, funk, rock, pop and reggae.

The backbone of any BBC local radio station is a fast and comprehensive news service, supported by reactive, topical programmes which develop the news and give listeners the opportunity to air their views. *The Breakfast Show* is broadcast from 6.30 to 9.00 a.m., Monday to Friday, followed by *Line Up* – affording listeners the opportunity to participate in debates on current issues, and put questions to people in authority (e.g. local MPs and municipal politicians), as well as professional experts, on such subjects as health, insurance, the law, social security and consumer affairs.

Radio Derby puts great store by its sports programmes, and over a three-year period has sold 8000 cassettes of its coverage of the fortunes of Derby County Football Club.

It is also part of Radio Derby's function to reflect, and where possible to encourage and stimulate local artistic activity. The station organises and promotes concerts throughout the area, including performances by the East of England Orchestra, and lunchtime recitals by up-and-coming artistes.

Occasionally, the lunchtime *Here & Now* programme serialises stories by local writers, and Radio Derby – together with Radios Leicester, Nottingham and Northampton – was associated with a recent Writer-in-Residence Fellowship, sponsored by East Midlands Arts, which culminated in the publication of an anthology of listeners' prose and poetry. Other than that there is not a great deal of scope for the broadcasting of written work within the popular 'sequence format' of Radio Derby's programmes. But if, having listened to Radio Derby, you feel you could make a useful written contribution, you should first of all telephone the Programme Organiser on (0332) 361111.

Radio Leicester

BBC Radio Leicester, the first local station in the United Kingdom, went on the air on 8 November 1967. It serves the county of Leicestershire (population 830,000) but is heard extensively beyond the county limit.

Greater Leicester, with its diverse industries, accounts for over half the population and in the city one in five is of Asian origin, but there is an extensive rural hinterland and several sizeable towns, Loughborough, Market Harborough, Coalville and Hinckley. The universities of Leicester and Loughborough and the Leicester Polytechnic are the area's major educational institutions.

Radio Leicester originates around ten hours per day of local output, shares a further two in the afternoon with the other East Midlands stations and is sustained through the night by Radio 2. Full-time staff number thirty-two and freelance contributors number at least two hundred.

Although music is not neglected, the main concern of the station is with lively and live speech. The breakfast programme reports the news and carries many interviews and 'packages' which reflect what is happening in the county. The mid-morning programme *Crosstalk* is a live phone-in/ magazine which relies heavily on attracting guests with something to say to the studio where they are invariably interviewed 'live'. Topics range from heated debates on local issues to specialist speakers on health, the law, education etc.

A range of specialist programmes cover topics as diverse as archaeology, religion, local music-making, gardening, transport. Five hours each week are given to the special needs of the Asian community and there are music programmes for country-and-western, jazz and folk enthusiasts.

Short stories and plays in a variety of Asian languages are broadcast from time to time and local writers are particularly encouraged by the Education Producer. Local authors are interviewed about their publications in *Crosstalk*. There is little scope, however, for the formal broadcast talk, with the exception of regular reviews of plays. Small fees are paid for short stories and commissioned work, but not for interviews.

Unsolicited material should be addressed to the Programme Organiser who will pass it on to the relevant producer.

Radio Lincolnshire

Radio Lincolnshire broadcast for the first time on 11 November 1980. It serves the fourth biggest county in the land and the largest editorial area of any of the BBC's stations – one and a half million acres with a population of more than half a million. A largely farming community with some industry along its western fringe, the county also includes the coastal resorts of Skegness and Mablethorpe.

The station originates more than eighty hours a week of its own programmes and each weekday afternoon links up for another two hours with the neighbouring stations at Nottingham, Derby and Leicester. Radio Lincolnshire has a staff of only twenty-two – among the smallest in local radio – but a number of part-time contributors from the community help to broaden the range of its programmes.

On weekdays the station relies on five main sequence programmes – the *Breakfast Show* (6.00–9.30 a.m.) with news,
sport, traffic news and a live link with the Nottingham Weather
Centre; the *Chris Jones Show* (9.30 a.m.–12.00 p.m.) which
includes a daily *Helpline* feature; *Midday* (12.00–2.00 p.m.), a
magazine programme which regularly comes from outside locations; *Afternoon Special* (2.00–4.00 p.m.) which is shared with
the neighbouring stations and features guests and phone-ins; a
tea-time sequence (4.00–7.00 p.m.) which features evening entertainment and events around the county.

At weekends the station's schedules include *Lincolnshire
Farming* (Friday 6.30–7.00 p.m., repeated Sunday 7.30 a.m.), a
religious magazine (Sunday 8.05 a.m.), a sports round-up (Friday 6.00 p.m.), an arts magazine and general documentaries.

While the station's limited staff and financial resources make it
difficult for Radio Lincolnshire to commit itself to many features
on a regular basis, it does welcome ad hoc contributions of local
interest.

Suggestions from contributors should be sent to the Programme Organiser. While reasonable expenses are normally
paid to contributors, the station has developed a number of
district studios in various main centres of population in order to
reduce the travelling difficulties created in a county the size of
Lincolnshire.

Radio Nottingham

BBC Radio Nottingham went on the air on 31 January 1968 and
covers central and South Nottinghamshire – a population of just
under a million. The area has a mixed economy, with mining and
more traditional forms of light engineering (e.g. Raleigh Industries) as well as science-based industries (Plessey and Boots).
Nottingham University is a well-established centre, and Trent
Polytechnic offers a wide range of facilities and courses. Nottingham has two successful theatres, and a thriving Concert Hall.
Outside the city at Holme Pierrepont is the National Water
Sports Centre, and there are several local football clubs with a
national reputation.

The station originates over seventy hours of local output each
week, but in addition provides another ten hours each week of a
programme jointly financed with Radios Derby, Leicester and
Lincolnshire. At other times the transmitters carry Radio 2.
There are thirty-one full-time members of staff, several others on
full-time contracts, and about another thirty regular programme
makers who contribute material on a weekly basis. Many others
assist more irregularly.

Radio Nottingham broadcasts a mixed speech and music output, although *Morning Report*, the breakfast programme, is
predominantly speech. It includes local and national affairs,

travel information, weather and a local 'What's On' service. John Simons' *Nottingham Connection* is a three-hour sequence daily from 9.05 a.m. to 12 noon, and is designed to respond to issues that may be raised by telephone or elsewhere. It increasingly carries feature material reflecting a wide range of contemporary issues. At 12.05 p.m. the mood changes with a more relaxing two-hour programme of music and entertainment hosted by Claire Catford. The East Midlands shared programme is hosted by Dennis McCarthy from 2.00 to 4.00 p.m. and achieves a large following for a highly individual mix of serious conversation and music. The *Weekday File* follows and as well as reflecting the day's news provides a fast moving mixture of guests, local events, an entertainment guide and travel information for those on the road or at home. At 6.00 p.m. there are specialist music programmes, more carefully directed for smaller audiences of highly motivated listeners. Weekend programmes are generally lighter and faster moving, the *Sunday Show* logging some of the highest figures recorded anywhere in the country.

Guests appear in all programmes. Those with special abilities and show business personalities are welcomed on to the *Afternoon Special* programme. Shorter items are also accommodated on the *Weekday File*, and those who may stimulate debate and discussion come into the *Nottingham Connection*. The station broadcasts some short stories, but few scripted talks, preferring to interview those who have experiences or knowledge worth sharing, often after the publication of a book or article. Scripts, tapes and cassettes are sent to the station in considerable numbers, and are given appropriate attention. Such items should be addressed to the Manager. All contributors receive their expenses, but fees are only paid to those who work for the station on a regular basis. Preference is given to contributors who live locally, or whose material reflects some aspect of local life.

Radio Shropshire

Radio Shropshire opened on 23 April 1985 covering the whole of England's largest inland county where almost half the population is in two centres – the ancient county town of Shrewsbury and the developing new town of Telford.

Local broadcasting, from a former supermarket on the northern outskirts of Shrewsbury, starts at 6.00 a.m. each weekday with a weekly total of over ninety hours of Shropshire-based output. While the regular programmes all have a music-speech mix, there is distinct bias in differing parts of the day. Music predominates between 9.00 a.m. and noon, and from 3.30 p.m. until close-down. The evenings, after 7.00 p.m., are given over to specialist music – country, classical, jazz and folk.

Two weekday programmes have a particular appeal for writers. From noon to 2.00 p.m., Chris Eldon Lee, in a virtually all-speech format, frequently interviews authors and looks at the world of books. That is followed by Diane Kemp's *Good Company* programme which works closely with arts organisations in Shropshire. Each afternoon, poets and authors air their work which should be under 1000 words, and is often read by the author. There is no restriction on topics, but local references and themes are given priority.

Scripts should be sent to the Programme Organiser, BBC Radio Shropshire, 2–4 Boscobel Drive, Shrewsbury SY1 3TT.

Radio Stoke

BBC Radio Stoke was launched back in the local radio experimental days of 1968, covering mainly the Potteries. Since then, its horizons have broadened to take in a wide area of North Staffordshire and South Cheshire, serving a population of around 750,000. The six towns that comprise the city of Stoke-on-Trent (Arnold Bennett forgot Fenton in his novels) are, of course, known worldwide for the quality of their ceramics. In addition, though, mining also plays an important part in the local economy. Once outside the city, agriculture is significant, as the environment becomes rapidly rural. This is an area of contrasts, from the sparsely-populated Staffordshire Moorlands to the rich dairylands of Cheshire.

Stoke's reputation as a city of smoke and grim slag heaps was once well-deserved. Now that's all changed because of far-reaching clean air policies and the most comprehensive land reclamation programme in Britain. Stoke and the surrounding area now enjoy a growing tourist industry based on industrial heritage. Museums such as the Chatterley Whitfield Mine and Gladstone Pottery provide a vivid record of traditional industries. The award-winning City Museum and the Wedgwood Visitors' Centre contain collections of the world's finest ceramics. The local network of canals was built for industrial usage in the eighteenth century. Indeed Josiah Wedgwood commissioned a canal to get his products to the ports in one piece. Today the waterways provide an excellent leisure facility.

BBC Radio Stoke has now become an integral part of this local fabric. The station broadcasts up to ninety hours a week of locally-originated programmes. The emphasis is on speech, which comprises about 65 per cent of the output. The aim is to reflect and report on the local community, with news and information playing an important part.

There is no regular programme for scripts, but prepared scripts are broadcast from time to time, usually within a magazine programme and when they are relevant to the locality. Although the station does not provide many outlets for writers, the Education Producer is always happy to be offered ideas and suggestions.

Radio WM (Birmingham and West Midlands)

Radio WM broadcasts to a potential three million listeners in and around the West Midlands. The editorial area includes parts of Warwickshire, Staffordshire and Hereford and Worcester. It is predominantly industrial, but the output of the station also reflects some of the more rural aspects of the West Midlands life as well as the unique cultures of its separate areas, Birmingham and the Black Country.

The station now broadcasts over one hundred hours of local material every week with a permanent staff of thirty-four. There is plenty of opportunity for freelance contributors and the station is always on the look-out for additional talents in this capacity.

Freelance writers are always of interest on Radio WM provided they are aiming their material at radio and not the written page. It also helps if it has some local interest, but that is not essential. The station does, however, use very little material from writers outside the area. Its greatest need is for short (three to five minute) local scripts to be read by the contributor. Some short stories are also used and humorous items are particularly welcome. The station is pleased to receive scripts and/or cassettes but recommends that writers should listen to its output before submitting any work. Any contributions used will be paid for. All material should be sent to the Manager.

BBC North East

BBC North East is the second largest of the new English Regions and serves a population of over eight million people east of the Pennines from the Scottish Border to the Wash. It comprises the two Television Centres at Leeds and Newcastle, and six BBC local radio stations – Cleveland, Humberside, Leeds, Newcastle, Sheffield and York. Newcastle's new Broadcasting Centre – home for Radio Newcastle since 1986 and for television since late 1987 – is one of the most modern in the country.

Television

Television production in the new region falls into three categories. The news and current affairs programme *Look North* is produced in separate nightly editions from Newcastle and Leeds and mainly relies on information and contributions from practising journalists. Each centre also produces a wide range of feature programmes for regional consumption, usually on the weekly Friday night BBC-2 slot. Thirdly, both centres produce some feature programmes for network screenings on BBC-1 or BBC-2, such as *An Ordinary Joe*, a profile of world snooker champion Joe Johnson (Leeds) and *Our Future We Build From The Past*, a powerful story of a Durham pit community in decline, or *The Man Who Made Beamish* (both Newcastle). Most of this work is commissioned and there are continuing opportunities for professional writers, particularly those living within the new region, to contribute to the output. Programme ideas, together with brief treatments, should be sent to the Head of Television at the BBC's Broadcasting Centre in Leeds or Newcastle.

Radio

Opportunities for new writers are perhaps greater in radio. During 1987, producer David Sheasby – himself a successful radio and television playwright – initiated a continuing project to develop the new region as a centre for radio writers. This is generating more material from the region for national radio broadcasts – including plays, short stories and arts features. New scripts and ideas should be sent to the Head of Radio Development at the BBC's Broadcasting Centre in Leeds. Individual stations also provide outlets for creative writing. Radio Leeds organises drama writing competitions, past winners of which have had their work produced for broadcast by Alan Ayckbourn. Radio Newcastle broadcasts locally written short stories and writing competitions. Radios Humberside and Sheffield also view the support of local writers as part of their wider role in reflecting and serving their local communities.

Radio Cleveland

Radio Cleveland, albeit under a different name, went on the air at midnight on 31 December 1970. It broadcasts to South Durham and North Yorkshire as well as Cleveland and to a population approaching three-quarters of a million.

It's an area of sharp economic and cultural contrasts. Cleveland is small but highly industrialised. North Yorkshire, or at least that part covered by Radio Cleveland, has wide farming areas and large tracts of moorland. County Durham also has its contrasts from the beauty of its Dales and Durham City, to the dereliction of former mining villages where pits have been closed as the economical coalfield moved under the sea. Unemployment, at the present time, is a major problem throughout all areas. Cleveland now has the highest unemployment rate of any county as its major chemical, steel and shipbuilding industries have contracted. Broadcasting, therefore, is of particular importance as a source of entertainment and information.

Radio Cleveland broadcasts its own programmes for an average of twelve hours a day. Outside this period, with the exception of Radio 1's *Top 40*, the station broadcasts Radio 2. To provide these services, there's a full-time staff of thirty-five plus freelance reporters and programme presenters.

Weekdays begin at 6.30 a.m. with *First Edition*. This three-hour 'breakfast magazine' reports on world, national and local

56

items of the day and provides an up-to-date weather, travel and local events information service. From 9.30 a.m. until 1.00 p.m. the listener has the opportunity to be entertained, to have a problem solved or express a view on a current topic in *Mainline*. The main news at 1 p.m. is followed by *Good Afternoon* until 4.00 p.m., a miscellany of what's going on in the area and the people who live in Cleveland or are passing through it. There are, of course, news bulletins on the hour throughout the day with a 'drive home' programme from 4.00 p.m. until 6.00 p.m.

Specialist programmes follow after 6.00 p.m. *Housecall*, on Tuesdays and Sundays, features listeners' poems, prose and letters. *Reach Out*, broadcast live on Wednesdays, takes a kaleidoscopic look at what's happening, going to happen or has happened in the arts. Thursday sees the *Focus on Folk* programme, often live, being transmitted from the studios in the centre of Middlesbrough. *Jhankar*, on Fridays, features the activities and musical tastes of Cleveland's Asian community, as well as highlighting topical items and local services of particular interest or importance to them.

The weekends really begin with *The Saturday Show*, an entertainment for all ages, followed by *Walkabout*, which features each week a local village or community. From 12 noon until 1.00 p.m. there's an alternative music programme which looks at local bands and groups and highlights their concerts.

Saturday Sport, at 2.00 p.m., follows the fortunes of Middlesbrough, Hartlepool, Darlington, Sunderland and Newcastle football clubs, as well as local rugby, racing, motor sport, athletics, cycling and ice hockey. At 8.05 a.m. on Sunday mornings local people share their ideas and talk about their Christian faith in *Right Lines*, followed at 8.20 a.m. by *Glorytime* – forty minutes of hymns of praise, songs of joy and other requests for sacred music. At 9.05 a.m. there's *Morning Sunday* – Radio Cleveland's 'colour' supplement.

At 11.30 a.m. *Dad's Music* combines the nostalgia of '78's with significant items from the last sixty years of local newspapers. There is one and a half hours of *Sunday Requests* over the lunch period, followed by another chance to hear *Housecall* and *Country Time*.

Radio Cleveland features local music of all styles, broadcast or recorded either on site, or in the station's new stereo-equipped studios. Schools are featured in the long-running *Top Team* quiz programme.

Among regular contributors to the station's programmes are experts on local history, astronomy, surnames, cooking, books and gardening. As a rule, interviews are preferred to a scripted format, with *Housecall* and certain special features the exceptions. Contributors write for this programme as a hobby – as no fees are paid. Items for consideration should be sent to the programme. All other programme contributions and suggestions should be addressed to the Programme Organiser.

Radio Humberside

Radio Humberside went on the air on 25 February 1971 and serves the population within the County of Humberside. The station's studio centre and newsroom are based in Hull, with a small satellite studio and staff of three in Grimsby, a news producer in Scunthorpe, and unattended studios in Beverley, Bridlington, Cleethorpes and Goole. The station produces twelve hours of local programmes each day and shares a total of eight and a half hours of specialist music programmes with BBC Radio Leeds, Sheffield and York.

Scripts, tapes and programme ideas, provided they are relevant to the area, are welcome and, if used, unsolicited material is paid for. Contributions should be sent to the Programme Organiser.

Radio Leeds

Radio Leeds is one of the BBC's pioneer local radio stations. Its success – together with that of the seven other experimental stations – convinced both the BBC and the then government that this new form of 'grass roots' public service radio should be encouraged to expand and ultimately become an indispensable feature of the nation's daily life.

Radio Leeds went on the air in June 1968. Originally located in a city centre shopping precinct, it soon outgrew its surroundings and in 1978 the development of a new site for BBC-TV provided the opportunity to move a few hundred yards up the road into the more spacious Broadcasting House – a landmark in Leeds associated with the BBC for many years.

More recently the station has greatly expanded its editorial boundaries from the city limits to take in all West Yorkshire. In 1981 it acquired stereo and thus became: Stereo Radio Leeds – the Voice of West Yorkshire.

The station finds itself in a county that regards itself as the heartland of the North and the east–west march of the Trans-Pennine motorway system has put the city of Leeds at the crossroads of the region. It has shown a better-than-average capacity for industrial survival and in times of economic difficulty has retained its position as a commercial centre. Local residents like to think of Leeds as the capital of the North, though this claim would certainly be challenged elsewhere.

The area served by Radio Leeds stretches from the Pennines in the West across forty miles of Yorkshire to the lush vale of York in the East. Between the two are more than two million people and an economy based on the historic industrial centres of Bradford, Huddersfield, Halifax and Wakefield. The textile industry continues to be a major employer, as does heavy and light engineering, printing and, in the south of the region, coal-mining. Agriculture, too, is a vital feature of West Yorkshire's economic life as is the newer industry of tourism since the area includes Ilkley Moor, the Pennines and the Brontë country. The Yorkshireman's love of sport is legendary and is represented in the reputation of the area's cricketers, and its rugby league and soccer teams.

West Yorkshire is also a centre of learning with universities in both Leeds and Bradford and specialisms in chemistry, medicine and technology. Leeds has one of the country's biggest Polytechnics whose reputation for the visual arts is worldwide. West Yorkshire also has a powerful musical tradition, particularly in the brass band world where Black Dyke Mills and the Yorkshire Imperial are household names. The Leeds International Pianoforte Competition is another of the region's prestige events and the International Print Biennale of Bradford has similar standing amongst artists.

BBC Radio Leeds tries to reflect this rich pattern of urban and rural life in its daily programmes, many of which are magazine sequences within which items can be as short as a minute or as long as a quarter of an hour. The accent of the programming is on speech with an overall speech to music ratio of 70:30. A significant development in the last two or three years has been the higher premium placed upon 'personality' presenters who can handle popular and fast-moving magazine programmes as well as more serious items. Such sequences occupy the high ground (i.e. 6.00 a.m.–6.00 p.m.) of the daily output whose backbone is news, current affairs and information.

Another recent development has been that of a daily Asian magazine programme, *Connections*, which is broadcast each weekday evening between 6.05 and 6.45 p.m., after which there are a variety of specialist programmes catering for jazz, classical music, folk, country, brass and rock enthusiasts. There are daily evening slots too, for 'access' programmes. Yorkshire's love of sport, and in particular rugby league and cricket, is legendary. Thus comprehensive sports reporting is an important component of the station's output, notably at weekends. For the last five years the station has held an open drama competition. Directors of winning entries have included Alan Ayckbourn and Alfred Bradley. The station is interested, too, in short stories and a range of other written contributions, though priority will always be given to local authors and writers. The expenses of contributors to programmes are paid provided that arrangements have been made beforehand. Scripts, tapes and cassettes should be sent to the station manager who will pass them to the individual producers.

Radio Newcastle

Radio Newcastle, which went on the air in January 1971, covers the largely urban and industrial county of Tyne and Wear, all of Northumberland and the northern end of County Durham. With a staff of thirty-six, the station is on the air roughly twelve hours a day, and also carries Radio 2 between 7.00 p.m. and 6.30 a.m.

Except for specially commissioned work, the station does not normally use the work of professional freelance writers although news items are used from bona fide journalists and these are paid for at the prevailing rates. However, as part of its role in encouraging local talent, Radio Newcastle does use a limited number of short stories from aspiring amateurs for which a small token payment is normally made. This material should be directed to the Programme Organiser or the Education Producer. Only material from local people is likely to be considered. There are occasional outlets for poetry by local people, but again only a token payment is likely.

Radio Sheffield

BBC Radio Sheffield is the second oldest local radio station, having opened in 1967. Currently, the station welcomes scripts especially for short stories which would normally be broadcast in the *Afternoon Edition* programme, an education based sequence programme broadcast on weekdays, 1.10–3.00 p.m.

Radio Sheffield occasionally broadcasts plays which are either by local authors or are about local issues, or both, but these are usually commissioned rather than sent in unsolicited.

Radio York

BBC Radio York opened on 4 July 1983 and broadcasts to an area stretching from Scarborough inland as far as Pateley Bridge at the edge of the Yorkshire Dales, and from Northallerton to Selby in the south. The population within Radio York's service area is around half a million.

North Yorkshire has a mixed economy and industrial base. To the south of the county, the Selby Coalfield is the largest and most modern in Europe. The coal produced is almost exclusively used by the giant power stations to the south of York. The City of York has a population of 100,000. Its main industries are chocolate manufacturing, railway engineering and tourism. Twenty-five miles to the West is Harrogate, a spa town and large commercial centre famous for its Conference Centre. Scarborough is a charming seaside town with a traditional fishing industry.

Radio York is very much a town and country station and is conscious of the need to reflect all elements of life within its large editorial area. With two national parks within North Yorkshire, Radio York is privileged to be the only local radio station serving this beautiful part of England.

The station broadcasts for approximately a hundred hours per week. Most of the staff are based in York but with such a large geographical area to cover, Radio York relies heavily on its remote studios in Malton, Harrogate, Scarborough, Selby, Northallerton and Thirsk. The Scarborough and Harrogate studios are particularly heavily used and each has a staff of three.

Radio York is always keen to receive short stories and features by local writers. Contributions set in or about the local area are of particular interest. The station retains the services of a literary adviser who reads all unsolicited scripts. The main outlet for local writers is within the *Mid-Morning* programme. Short stories of under six minutes duration are especially suitable. Feature material is also welcome, although generally this is best treated in a more imaginative way than a straight read to microphone. Such scripts therefore often form the basis of a researched local feature or series so long as the subject is of strong local relevance.

Contributions should be sent to the Programme Organiser.

BBC North West

The North West region with a population of over seven million stretches from Greater Manchester across to Merseyside and Cheshire, and includes Lancashire, the Lake District and Cumbria.

The former Manchester Network Production Centre is the nucleus – and a major feature in terms of both employment opportunities and programme ideas – of the newly-created BBC North West, which includes the current Network Television and Network Radio Production Centre, the regional television operation, and four local radio stations: BBC Radio Cumbria, Lancashire, Manchester and Merseyside.

The integration of all the BBC's broadcasting activities in the North West region has provided opportunities for greater mobility between programme areas, an enhanced news-gathering operation and an increased profile for the Corporation in the region. By effectively handling its resources the new region is able both to plan innovatively and to reinforce existing strengths. At the same time, it aims to attract able and talented people to the North West region. The combination of network television and radio, regional television and local radio under a unified management structure presents increased opportunities for further development.

Network Television

BBC North West currently makes about 350 programmes a year for BBC-1 and BBC-2 and is one of the most productive of all the Regions. Productions are many and various but output is concentrated in four main areas – Sport, Entertainment, Features and

Children's programmes. The Sports Department is responsible for all the BBC's snooker and darts coverage as well as major contributions to cricket, bowls and racing. It produces *A Question of Sport*, one of BBC TV's most popular quiz programmes. Entertainment from Manchester includes *No Limits*, the rock magazine programme, *Red Dwarf*, the new futuristic BBC comedy series, *Harty*, which takes Russell Harty to all corners of the world, and *Fax*, the fun information programme.

The North West can now claim to be the main current affairs centre outside London with its flagship series *Brass Tacks*, winner in 1985 of the Royal Television Society award for Best Current Affairs Programme. *Open Air* encourages viewers to talk back to programme makers and *The Travel Show* provides regular information for holiday plans.

In Children's programmes BBC North West produces the Saturday Morning Show *It's Wicked* every summer weekend and other programmes for the very young as well as the religious programme for young people *Umbrella*.

Network Radio

Network Radio presents probably the best opportunities for writing talent. BBC North West in Manchester is the largest supplier of programmes for Radio 1, 2, 3 and 4 outside London, providing more than 1300 hours of programmes for the national networks. Producers cover the whole spectrum of broadcasting – light entertainment, serious and light music, drama, talks and current affairs, features and documentaries and a rich concentration of outside radio broadcasts.

BBC North West has long had a considerable reputation as the single biggest patron of new drama writing in the North and has been responsible for developing the talents of new writers to stand alongside such names as Alan Bleasdale, Brian Thompson, Alan Plater and Barry Hines. The recent refurbishment of the radio drama studio will add to the number and quality of programmes produced in Manchester – programmes such as *Saturday Night Theatre*, *The Monday Play* and *The Afternoon Play*. A mark of the encouragement of northern writers is the 6000 and more scripts received by the six regular drama producers. Future plans include the involvement of local students in attending radio production rehearsals (discussing techniques in writing, performance and direction) and a workshop for local writers, actors and producers to investigate new ideas and seek ways of nurturing a lively local community of radio drama.

Regional Television

The mainstay of regional programmes is the nightly weekday news magazine programme *North West Tonight*. This seeks to reflect the richness and diversity of events and activities in the region and since it is news based, relies mainly on contributions from journalists, but ideas for news and feature items are welcome. Topical appeal is an advantage, but there is no restriction on subject matter, other than that it has regional significance. The programme uses a modern television studio, a two-camera lightweight outside broadcast unit and portable single camera (PSC) video.

Forty half-hour regional feature programmes are made each year, ranging from documentaries (*A Ken Russell Picture – Song of the Lakes*); light entertainment (*Top Town*, a TV talent show); general interest programmes (*Now*, in which Russell Harty tours the region meeting personalities and discussing topical issues) and in-depth looks at matters of regional concern (e.g. a programme examining the aftermath of the Abbeystead explosion). The scope of the output is deliberately wide-ranging. A summary of an idea or an outline treatment should be sent before a full script. Material should be sent to, Manager TV Production, BBC North West, Oxford Road, Manchester M60 1SJ.

Regional Radio

File on 4, Radio 4's principal current affairs documentary, is produced in Manchester and the weekly programmes examine the background to current events at home and abroad. The quality and range of the feature and documentary output includes *You'll Never be Sixteen Again*, a history of the British teenager; the discussion programme *A Word in Edgeways*; *Gardeners' Question Time*, which recently celebrated its fortieth anniversary; and the series of 'fly on the wall' documentaries *Actuality*.

Many of the programmes produced by the features team are generated by local writers. *Solomon Grundy, Inside Job, Waiting for Mrs Forbes* and a wide range of talks are produced relying on people with something to say and the ability to say it well.

In comedy and light entertainment, the heritage of the northern comedy circuit and the strength, variety and availability of so much local writing ability have resulted in a stream of material. *The Grumbleweeds, Castle's Corner*, Les Dawson, Ken Dodd, Jimmy Jewell and Max Wall are established favourites. Recent successes have been *Back to Square One* – a new quiz show for Radio 2 – and *Living with Betty* – a new situation comedy. New writers able to contribute short sketches or whole scripts are always sought, especially in the area of contemporary comedy.

Another recent development is *Cat's Whiskers* on Radio 4, which seeks to encourage children raised on a diet of television, to listen to the radio. Suggestions for other radio forms, especially in drama, which will encourage and satisfy younger listeners are welcome.

Ideas for programmes in all areas should be sent to the Head of Network Radio, BBC North West, Oxford Street, Manchester M60 1SJ.

Radio Cumbria

Radio Cumbria, which originally opened on 24 November 1973 as BBC Radio Carlisle, serves roughly the northern half of Cumbria including the towns of Carlisle, Brampton, Maryport, Workington, Whitehaven, Keswick, Penrith and Appleby. Within this area there is an adult population of approximately 300,000 and a very large farming audience, but it also contains heavy industry in the west with British Steel, Leyland Truck and Bus, B.N.F.L. and Marchon Chemicals among many others. There are few overseas immigrants in the area but a large number of people visit it for a short time for the purposes of tourism and in consequence there is a large number of hotels.

In late May 1982, BBC Radio Furness opened in Barrow, serving the southern part of the county, and it was then that Radio Carlisle changed its name to BBC Radio Cumbria. Radio Furness carries Radio Cumbria programmes, opting out for up to an hour a day for its own local news and information programme. This has increased the Radio Cumbria audience to approximately 650,000 and its editorial area to the whole of Cumbria. The topography of the region causes some reception difficulties so that there are 'pockets' in the centre of the county that do not have satisfactory reception. The change to Radio Cumbria brought into the editorial area the heavy industry of Barrow – shipbuilding, chemicals, engineering – and the large farming and tourist area of the Southern Lakes and Morecambe Bay.

Currently Radio Cumbria originates approximately seventy hours of output each week, carrying Radio 2 at other times. It has a staff of thirty-one full-time employees and two part-timers. Radio Furness opened with a staff of four. The programmes of Radio Cumbria are like those of most other local radio stations with news and information providing the 'bread and butter' of the output. Starting at 6.30 in the morning a pattern of sequence broadcasting takes the station to the early evening at which point programmes of more specialist interest, including young people's and farming programmes, predominate. At weekends information and sport are most important but there is then opportunity for documentary, light entertainment and local music programmes.

The mid-morning sequence, *Open Air*, and the early afternoon programme, *1–2–3*, both welcome contributions from outside. These may be in the form of short stories, written features or poetry, sometimes with an emphasis on local dialect but not necessarily so. It is important, however, that opportunities should first be provided for local writers or contributions should have at least their roots in Cumbria. According to the nature of the item it may be read by the writer or by a member of the staff. The collaboration of local writers in the making of feature or documentary programmes outside the magazine format is also welcomed.

In recent years Radio Cumbria has participated in the North-West Radio Play-writing Competition along with BBC Radios Merseyside, Manchester, Stoke and Lancashire.

Unsolicited tapes and cassettes are welcome as well as scripts and should be sent to the Programme Organiser. The station pays for contributions and also reimburses the reasonable expense of contributors visiting the station to broadcast.

Radio Lancashire

Radio Lancashire replaced Radio Blackburn, which had then been broadcasting to the people of North-East Lancashire for ten years, in July 1981. It was intended to serve the 1.3 million population within the new boundaries of the county prescribed by Local Government Reorganisation in 1974, when Manchester and Merseyside became metropolitan counties in their own right and the Furness district became part of Cumbria.

Lancashire is now a compact county – roughly forty miles long by thirty miles wide, bounded by the Irish Sea to the west and the Yorkshire Pennines to the east. Most people live in the industrial belt in the south – the old cotton towns of Preston, Chorley, Blackburn, Burnley, now no longer dependent on the vestigial cotton trade although still pioneering new textiles and the machinery to produce them. Electronics, plastics, paper, aircraft, commercial vehicles, furniture, bedding, wall coverings have all been developed to beat the decline in cotton.

But four-fifths of the county is rural, with a coastline which attracts millions of visitors each year. In addition to world-famous Blackpool there are also the 'gentler' resorts of Lytham St Annes, Cleveleys and, to the north, Morecambe. The rivers Ribble, Hodder and Lune not only provide marvellous fishing, but flow through some of the most attractive valleys in England. The M6 and the West Coast main railway line neatly mark the divide between the hills and moors to the east and the broad, rich plains to the west growing the root crops and tomatoes which supply most of the North-West. Indeed it was the abundance of potatoes from the Fylde which were married to the plentiful fish landed at Fleetwood which produced the first, and perhaps most lasting, convenience food, fish and chips, which fed generations of millworkers. The area also contains Lancaster University and Lancashire Polytechnic and is notable for a tradition of fierce independence and local pride.

Radio Lancashire provides about ninety hours of local broadcasting each week. Most of the output is a mixture of news, information and music. However, poems and short stories are always welcome for the monthly programme *Your Chapter and Verse* broadcast on the fourth Sunday each month. It is not necessary to live in Lancashire to submit scripts, but it *is* necessary to have strong connections with the county. Competition is fierce, and at the time of writing, the programme would have enough material to keep it going for the next four years even if it received no more scripts during that time. Submissions for *Your Chapter and Verse* should be sent to the producer.

Radio Manchester

Radio Manchester has steadily enhanced its programme range since it opened in 1970 and today has probably the widest spread of ethnic minority programmes in local radio.

Ironically, it was through its newest ethnic minority programme that the station reached its biggest potential audience. When *Eastern Horizon*, broadcasting to the 30,000 Chinese in the North West, linked up by satellite with Radio Beijing for a Chinese New Year 'special', the programme was relayed to nearly one billion Chinese listeners in the Chinese Republic and worldwide. *Eastern Horizon* joins the station's long-running *Eastwards Northwestwards*, broadcasting to the region's Asian community, and the Afro-Caribbean magazine, *I'n'I Rule OK*. Manchester's oldest ethnic strand – the Irish – also have their own night-time slot, *Come Into the Parlour*.

Radio Manchester's specialist music programmes are even more varied. They range from country, jazz, organ music, folk, soul, classical music, rock'n'roll and new wave. Local musician Jenny McKenzie, who presents a classical music hour each week, has also presented a showcase series for local musicians of all kinds. The station's day-time sequences present a mix of chart music, plus '60s and '70s nostalgia.

For all its specialist programme strands, the station relies on a small army of volunteer presenters and production staff to augment its own staff of more than thirty. There is a special programme for and by disabled people, another for anglers, yet another for ramblers and nature lovers, an *Action Line* team working on community projects, and a religious affairs team which has broadened its scope to look at social issues as well as matters relating directly to the Church. The same team produce and present a late-night Sunday problem phone-in, which has won awards for its innovative ideas.

News is a vital strand in the station's output and as well as supplying regular bulletins on the hour – and more often at peak times – the newsroom is a source of dozens of features every day, plus 'specials' such as a nuclear arms debate with a studio audience and national political figures taking part.

Radio Manchester producers are always open to receive feature and programme ideas – a phone call, letter or a press release will usually suffice – but the market for written material is limited. The station now runs its own play-writing competition, with the best two plays being broadcast by Radio Manchester and possibly syndicated to other stations in the region. Anyone wanting to submit a play, any other written material or a programme idea should contact the Programme Organiser.

Radio Merseyside

BBC Radio Merseyside went on the air on 22 November 1967. Fourteen years later, on 7 December 1981, a brand-new radio station opened in Liverpool's Paradise Street – the first purpose-built BBC local radio station. Editorially, its area stretches from Southport to Chester, from Warrington to the River Dee. There is also a healthy listenership in North Wales, in the main ex-Merseysiders and commuters.

Such a large area takes in every aspect of community life. Liverpool is a major city and port, an industrial centre, currently experiencing high unemployment. There is a university and several colleges of further education. The city has a large and well-established Chinese population, a thriving Asian community, Toxteth, with its second- and third-generation blacks. Southport, to the north, is a seaside resort catering for many retired people and – in the summer – for an influx of holidaymakers. Chester, in the south, has its historical remains – and its barracks. There is farming in Wirral and north-west Lancashire; there is also Warrington, Widnes, St Helens, Birkenhead and the new towns of Runcorn and Skelmersdale.

BBC Radio Merseyside broadcasts for some 120 hours each week with a staff of thirty-five. Freelance contributors are employed to compile and present specialist programmes – music, countryside matters, the arts and so on.

The station offers a wide range of programmes. A strong emphasis on news and current affairs is tempered by music of every kind (jazz, country, folk, classical, Asian, big band, rock, disco, brass), drama and talks, outdoor pursuits, local history, sport, religion, humour, quizzes, and magazines for the immigrant populations.

There are four major daily sequence programmes: *Morning Merseyside*, on weekdays from 6.00–8.30 a.m.; *The Billy Butler Show*, on weekdays from 8.30–11.30 a.m.; this includes the award-winning *Helpful Hour* offering advice and practical help to charities, the disabled etc., encouraging listeners to help others; *Town And Around*, on weekdays from 11.30–2.00 p.m., including music, news and current affairs, consumer and legal advice, the 'newsline' phone-in offering listeners the chance to comment on current topics; Debi Jones on weekdays from

3.05–6.00 p.m., including music, guests, news and sport, traffic and travel etc.

Other successful programmes include *Merseyside Sports Special* – this is a major sporting area – on Saturdays at 2.30 p.m., and *Streetlife*, a Sunday evening show for those between fifteen and twenty-five.

Outside contributions (other than programmes actually put together by regular freelances) are accepted by *First Heard*, a fortnightly half-hour of stories by local writers. There is also *Late Night Story*, a five- to ten-minute story broadcast in the *Sunday Late Show* each week. *First Heard Poetry* is an occasional edition of *First Heard*, this time composed entirely of poetry from local writers. Stories are sometimes read by the authors, more often by professional or semi-professional readers; poetry is never read by its author. The station does not welcome unsolicited cassettes or tapes. Contributions used on air are paid for. Material should be sent to the Editor, *First Heard/Late Night Story* or the Editor, *First Heard Poetry*.

There is a daily religious *Talking Point*. Contributions for this should go to the presenter.

South and East

By the creation of the South and East Region the BBC has, for the first time, made a commitment to provide a proper regional service for the millions living in London and the South-East. The new Region, the largest and most densely populated of the five English Regions, stretches from The Wash to Sussex and from the North Sea to Oxfordshire. It encompasses fourteen counties. The Head of Broadcasting (South and East) and his management team have their headquarters at the BBC's Elstree Centre in Borehamwood, Herts.

At the same time as creating the Region, the BBC has given it an important role in network production. Much of the output formerly produced by Network Features and Outside Broadcast Entertainments has been transferred to the Region. The History and Archaeology and General Programmes Units are now based at Elstree, as is the team responsible for *Global Report*. *Timewatch* is the principal strand of the History and Archaeology Unit, which also makes series such as *Footsteps* and *The Great Journeys*. The General Programmes Unit has taken over the popular quizzes *Mastermind* and *Masterteam*, produces *Children in Need* and other appeals, and makes specialised chess and bridge programmes. New ideas to enhance the Region's network role should be submitted to the Head of Television (South and East) at Elstree.

Production of regional programmes for London and the South-East is split between Elstree and Lime Grove. In the longer term the nightly news magazine *London Plus* will move to Elstree but for the time being it continues to be produced from Lime Grove, although it is a Regional responsibility. During 1988/9 the region will embark on the production of forty Regional features for the BBC-2 opt-out slot, a substantial increase on the twenty-four to thirty produced in 1987/8. The Editor Television, South-East, has recently been appointed to take overall responsibility for *London Plus*, to edit the opt-out programmes and to maximise any network opportunities which arise. Since there is no tradition of opt-out programmes for London and the South-East, there is no set format. Ideas for one-off programmes or for short series reflecting aspects of life in this diverse and busy area will be welcomed by the Editor Television, South-East, at Elstree.

In contrast to London and the South-East, the Eastern counties have enjoyed a proper regional service for many years. The Norwich Studio Centre employs around 100 people on the production of *Look East*, the nightly BBC-1 news magazine which follows the *Six o'Clock News*; a Saturday sports and news spot; forty BBC-2 opt-out programmes per year under the umbrella title of *East on Two*; and a number of networked documentaries, which have earned a high reputation for the Norwich production team. These have recently included the award-winning *The Dying Swan* and the controversial Easter feature *England's Nazareth* about the shrines at the Norfolk village of Little Walsingham. The Region is always interested in ideas both to fit in with the current output or for new series. Ideas which can make the most of the present small studio are particularly welcome. Please contact the Television Manager, East, at Norwich.

Unlike the other Regions, the South and East plays no part in network radio production. The Region is responsible, however, for nine local radio stations – BBC Radio Bedfordshire, Cambridgeshire, Essex, Kent, London, Norfolk, Northampton, Oxford and Sussex. Ideas for individual stations should be submitted to the relevant station Manager. The Head of Local Radio (South and East) is always interested in ideas with a wider application; he is based at Elstree.

Radio Bedfordshire

Radio Bedfordshire came on-air on 24 June 1985. It covers the whole of Bedfordshire, North Buckinghamshire (including Milton Keynes) and North and West Hertfordshire, which totals approximately 1.4 million people. This is a heavily urbanised area with large numbers of commuters to London but retains wide tracts of green fields though few are actually employed in rural industry any longer. There is a heavy reliance on London and little parochial interest beyond the actual town that people live in. The radio station is based in Luton which is the focal centre for what is in essence a sub-region. Other major towns include Bedford, Milton Keynes, Stevenage and St Albans. Employment ranges from Vauxhall Motors in Luton to Texas Instruments in Bedford and a range of high tech industries in the new towns of Buckinghamshire and Hertfordshire. The character of the area is increasingly determined by the effect of transport and commuting – the M1, the A1 and three main London passenger train lines run through the area.

Radio Bedfordshire employs thirty-five people, two-thirds of whom are on the editorial staff producing over 100 hours of locally originated broadcasting each week. When not broadcasting its own material (usually from 10.00 p.m. to 6.00 a.m. overnight) the station carries Radio 2.

The station's daytime material is a 70:30 speech to music mix with a heavy emphasis on news and current affairs but encompassing a wide range of feature material within the station output. The music is tuneful, melodic and familiar, appealing to the over thirty-five age bracket, while the station's speech component includes a wide variety of contributions from members of the local community. Particularly in the evenings for the ethnic communities – who form a large percentage of the population of Luton and Bedford and receive fifteen hours of programmes per week for the Asian, Afro-Caribbean and Italian communities. At the weekend there are opportunities for local contributions in a written form. The station is keen to explore the rich vein of historical material and the writing skills of local amateurs usually in the form of short talks which may or may not be illustrated at a duration of no more than five minutes. Submissions are welcomed, though the take up rate is naturally limited to suitable programme areas. The usual week of broadcasting will contain one or two contributions of this type made, normally, on an expenses only basis. All submissions should have a local content.

Radio Cambridgeshire

The station went on the air on 1 May 1982. It covers the whole of this East Anglian county which was formed in 1974 by the amalgamation of the two counties of Cambridgeshire and the Isle of Ely, and Huntingdon and Peterborough: an area of more than 1300 square miles with a population of just over half a million. The main centres of population are the university city of Cambridge and the rapidly developing new town of Peterborough: two cities of great contrast.

Although there has been increasing housing, commercial and industrial development in recent years in the western half of the county, particularly in Peterborough and the Ouse Valley towns, Cambridgeshire remains predominantly rural. Farmers own or control more than eighty per cent of the land in the county (compared to the average of seventy per cent in England and

Wales) and the quality of the area's arable farming is internationally recognised. Since the flat, austere Fens in the North-East were reclaimed by drainage in the seventeenth and eighteenth centuries, they have become what is perhaps the best expanse of arable land in the country. Industrially, Cambridgeshire has become famous for medical science and for the work of specialised technological research and development agencies and organisations. Industrial and scientific connections with agriculture are widespread and significant.

The county town of Cambridge is a cosmopolitan and sophisticated place whose most obvious characteristics are the splendid colleges, narrow streets, tourists and bicycles. But the city's industry, though unobtrusive, is extensive and includes printing, scientific instrument making, flour milling, asphalt manufacture, cement working and electronics.

In the north, Peterborough feels more like an East Midlands industrial city than a part of a rural county. It is the focus of important road and rail services and a bustling commercial and agricultural base dominated by engineering, textiles manufacture, sugar beet farming and a large brickworks. Other principal centres include the expanding towns of Huntingdon and St Neots – which have grown largely because of the planned influx of Londoners and London industry – and the cathedral city of Ely and the inland port of Wisbech. Huntingdon is often remembered as the birthplace of Oliver Cromwell, and Robin Hood figures in some later versions of his legend as the Earl of Huntingdon. Wisbech is a market town and municipal borough as well as a port, and, like Huntingdon, is mainly agricultural. It is notable for its cattle markets, canning works, fruit and vegetable farms, engineering, brewing, printing and basketmaking. Its School of Horticulture was the first of its kind in England. The county was the pioneer in the establishment of the Village College, based upon the philosophy of William Morris.

In serving such a polyglot community one has to take account of industrial workers, bulb-growers, scientists, engineers, university dons, fen farming folk and a host of workers in the professional and service industries.

Radio Cambridgeshire provides ninety hours of locally produced programmes each week with a staff of thirty. In addition there is a small army of contributors who broadcast on specialist topics within magazine programmes or help with outside broadcasts as additional interviewers or with technical assistance.

During the evening, the station relays Radio 2 – although more of its own programmes are being transmitted in the evening as resources allow. Two notable examples are a rock music show which is also broadcast by two neighbouring BBC Stations on Sunday evenings, and a ninety-minute music and information magazine for Asian listeners on Thursday evenings.

The most fruitful area for aspiring contributors in terms of writing for the station lies in historical research. The station has produced several series centred on specific themes of the present century. The station also co-sponsors and runs an annual short story competition, of which the winning entries are broadcast.

Reviewers of films, books, plays, concerts and the like who are also good broadcasters are welcomed, as writers of drama and above all light entertainment would be, if the resources were available. Essentially the subject matter should reflect Cambridgeshire life, customs, people and humour.

Contributors should contact the Programme Organiser.

BBC Essex

BBC Essex began broadcasting in November 1986 and its area is the whole county of Essex – from the London suburbs in the west to the coastal resorts of Clacton and Frinton in the east, and from the pretty East Anglian villages in the north down to the industrial Thames estuary in the south.

Essex is a county of great contrasts and the radio station tries to reflect this in its speech programming. For example, it is interested in preserving the memory of the rural past and the old Essex dialect but it is just as concerned to delve into the problems of contemporary urban existence.

The radio station is based in the county town of Chelmsford at the pivotal point where Metropolitan Essex starts becoming East Anglian Essex.

Unsolicited scripts must be on an Essex theme. They should be addressed to the Programme Organiser at 198 New London Road, Chelmsford CM2 9XB.

The station does not use unsolicited material regularly but nevertheless it encourages local writers to submit their work for consideration.

Radio Kent

BBC Radio Kent, formerly Radio Medway, first went on the air in December 1970. The station changed its name in 1983 and expanded its editorial area to take in the whole of Kent. Thus with manned studios in Chatham, Canterbury, Maidstone and Tonbridge, Radio Kent provides news and information and a wide range of programmes to a potential audience of one and a half million people.

News bulletins and material in magazine programmes reflect the fact that Kent is a diverse county with interests ranging from high tech industry to farming, from leisure and tourism to shipping and ferry ports which handle more than twenty million passengers a year. Radio Kent's output also provides information at regular intervals for the county's many road and rail commuters. To assist the gathering of news and views across a county covering 1400 square miles there are unmanned studios in Dartford, Gravesend, Ashford, Dover, Sittingbourne, Tunbridge Wells and Margate, and a network of volunteer village correspondents. Further contribution studios are planned for Folkestone, which will be closely involved in any development of a Channel Tunnel, and Sevenoaks.

Radio Kent broadcasts more than 100 hours of local programmes a week, presented by staff or paid freelancers, and is on the air on weekdays from 6.00 a.m. to 10.00 p.m. with a slight variation of hours at weekends. At breakfast time and towards lunchtime the main emphasis is on news and current affairs, topical talking points and expert advice. The aim in the early afternoon is to offer Kent a countywide noticeboard for events, and at other times programmes seek to provide local interest, humour and entertainment, phone-in debates and specialist music.

Theatrical and literary endeavour are reflected in the weekly programme *Scene and Heard* (Tuesdays at 7.00 p.m.). Short illustrative extracts are featured, though in the main, the programme involves writers, performers and producers discussing their work, often from the stage door on opening night. The amateur stage gets a fair look-in, too. Reflecting the work of local writers, however, is not the sole preserve of the Arts programme, and some are the subject of feature interviews in magazine programmes.

So far as encouraging the work of amateur writers is concerned Radio Kent now welcomes poetry and rhyme contributions from the 'scribblers for fun'. In *People to People* (Mondays to Fridays at 3.00 p.m.) and *Sunday Special*, Gerry Savage features listeners' poems and rhyme, lighthearted or serious or otherwise, the aim being to provide a little encouragement and wider exposure through a brief broadcast. The station also offers occasional poetry programmes, the most recent reflecting thoughts of Christmas and Easter.

Radio Kent is currently exploring ways to encourage further work in poetry and prose, possibly through poetry and short story competitions in 1988.

Unless unsolicited material is directed at specific programme outlets, it is difficult to respond adequately, but so far as unsolicited material is concerned the chief criteria in assessment will be topicality and the local interest potential for a Kent audience.

Radio London

Radio London first broadcast on 6 October 1970. In theory the listeners were to be the people who live in the City and the thirty-two boroughs within the administrative boundary of London. In practice the station has attracted many of its listeners from the Home Counties, not least because of the first-class travel service for commuters and motorists broadcast all through the day. There are twelve million people living within reach of Radio London's transmitters.

The station broadcasts 120 hours a week from its own studios and when not originating programmes carries Radio 2, this is usually from around midnight to 6.30 a.m. There are about forty-three staff working in the studios in Marylebone High Street, with about thirty on contract or working as freelancers.

About 50 per cent of Radio London's output is music, with the emphasis very much on music generated within the capital itself. As one end of the musical spectrum, the station has carried four concerts from the Messiaen Festival set up by the Royal Academy of Music, and others from the graduates of the London Music Colleges banded together in the Young Musicians' Symphony Orchestra. Radio London also carries all kinds of specialist 'pop' music, usually live and made on the streets of London, including 'soul', 'funk', 'jazzbop' and 'rap'. Much of this material is provided by live or recorded concerts which the station itself has promoted.

A great part of the rest of the station's effort goes into news, in the broadest sense of the word. At breakfast time there is *Rush-Hour*; news, information, a comprehensive travel service, and interviews and reports that keep the Londoner right up-to-date with what's happening in his city and round the world. There are news bulletins all through the day. There are nightly documentaries reflecting current affairs, politics, the arts and sport in the capital. There is also a weekly half-hour about London's government.

The station prides itself on its reaction to the unexpected or the emergency. This has included special programmes on the Broadwater Farm riots; live, full-length broadcasts of parliamentary debates on the demise of the Greater London Council and the problems of pensioners in London; and a night-long results programme on the last London Borough elections.

Every night Radio London broadcasts *Black Londoners*, an hour-long programme which, as its name implies, is primarily of interest to the city's black population. This is a wide-ranging programme covering politics, the arts, sport, music, and Caribbean affairs; and it encourages young people in the skills of broadcasting. Two programmes are broadcast for London's Asian community, on Saturday and Sunday evenings, and there are also two weekly programmes for the Jewish community, one of which has already been running for fifteen years.

Radio London welcomes contact with its listeners and contributions from them, though most of these are informal participation in phone-ins, quizzes and music programmes. At weekends listeners hear from Londoners who have organised local events.

It is very seldom that the station uses unsolicited scripts. It is unprecedented, as well, for a presenter to have been recruited from an unsolicited cassette – though one or two people have come quite near it. It would be a dull radio station, though, that forbade its listeners to try their luck.

Radio Norfolk

Radio Norfolk began broadcasting on 11 September 1980 and serves the whole of the county of Norfolk and the Waveney Valley area of north Suffolk, three-quarters of a million people. Although agriculture is no longer the biggest employer, farming is Norfolk's most obvious activity and many people in its scattered villages earn their living from associated industries. More than half the population live in small village communities. Only Norwich, with a population of 125,000, can be described as a big city, King's Lynn, Yarmouth and Lowestoft can be considered large towns. The only other places with a population of more than 10,000 are Dereham and Thetford.

Probably the biggest employer is the holiday industry which is expanding into the rural areas with developments like horse-drawn caravan holidays and bird-watching expeditions. The traditional Broads holidays also attract many visitors as do the coastal resorts like Yarmouth and Cromer. This part of East Anglia is growing in population at a greater rate than almost any other part of the country, with retired people making up the greatest proportion of these new residents.

Industrially there is an almost complete mix with everything from a small motor car industry to heavy electrical factories via microprocessors, and boots and shoes. The University of East Anglia at Norwich is the major cultural centre of the area.

Radio Norfolk employs twenty-six people full-time, half of whom are editorial staff, and five freelance presenters on a part-time basis. Between them they produce 110 hours of locally originated broadcasting a week. When not broadcasting its own material, the station carries Radio 2.

The general output of the station is similar to that network in style and content. Its programmes are 95 per cent live and almost totally unscripted. It broadcasts contributions from local writers, but almost always in interview form (for which fees are not normally paid, though expenses are often met) Occasionally, local amateurs contribute stories and poems which they read at the microphone, but these are not usually of more than five minutes' duration, and again these broadcasts are made on an expenses only basis.

Radio Northampton

Radio Northampton first began broadcasting in 1982 and its programmes of news, information, entertainment and music quickly made it a firm favourite among listeners, from the former steel town of Corby in the north-east of the county to the more rural area of Brackley in the south-west of Northamptonshire.

The station has manned studios at Corby and Wellingborough, along with studio facilities in Kettering, Towcester and Daventry. The station uses these facilities combined with a radio car to enable a great variety of programmes to come from all over the country. The usual broadcasting hours are from 6.00 a.m. to 10.00 p.m. on weekdays and from 7.00 a.m. to 8.00 p.m. at weekends.

In 1987 Radio Northampton received a Sony nomination for its *Celebration of Christmas* Outside Broadcast programme, scripted by local freelance broadcaster David Saint. A comedy series was added to the output in autumn 1987.

The station is part of the BBC's South and East region but retains its links with the group of stations which have combined with East Midlands Arts to produce poetry and short story competitions. Schools have also been ecouraged to participate through the Local Education Authority's liaison officer.

Programmes range through news and current affairs, consumer matters and the general day-to-day life of the county and its people to more specialist broadcasting on music, the arts and youth.

Radio Oxford

BBC Radio Oxford went on the air in October 1971. It serves the entire county of Oxfordshire and a large part of West Buckinghamshire (the Aylesbury/Buckingham area). Outside Oxford itself, with its famous University and almost equally well-known car works, the area is predominantly farmland, and a conscious effort is made to broadcast to the farming community and to the many thousands of people who live in the villages. The station broadcasts its own programmes for approximately eighty-four hours a week. It uses Radio 2 throughout the night. The staff number thirty-two.

The station's weekday output is largely divided into major sequences as follows:

(1) 6.00 a.m.– 9.00 a.m. *Oxford AM*. Beginning as a music/speech mix programme, *Oxford AM* develops into a news and current affairs breakfast show with many regular features.
(2) 9.00 a.m.– 12.00 p.m. The mid-morning sequence, *Open Air*, is presented by Mark Kasprowicz and covers issues of national and local importance. There is good music plus phone-ins and light-hearted quizzes.
(3) The sequences are broken at midday by a variety of other programmes, such as *Just the Job, My Choice, In the Country, Tunes Remembered* and *People and Places*.

(4) 3.30 p.m.– 6.00 p.m. A fast-moving 'drive-time' programme, presented by Geraldine McCullagh.

On Saturday mornings, both *Oxford AM* and *Open Air* have their sixth editions, but each has a lighter flavour. The afternoon is taken up with sport and music.

Programmes for Sundays include the popular *Spirit Level* religious magazine programme, a request show, an Arts programme and others, reflecting both the Afro-Caribbean and Asian communities in the Oxford area. During term time Oxford University undergraduates also have their own programme on a Sunday afternoon.

Radio Sussex

BBC Radio Sussex broadcasts for an average of twelve hours per day to the population of the two counties of East and West Sussex. The market for scripted material is, as with all local stations, strictly limited by shortage of resources and suitable programme opportunities. The station does, however, produce several radio plays every year. The scripts for these plays are normally drawn from the entries to a playwriting competition organised in conjunction with South East Arts, and launched at a radio drama seminar in the spring. These seminars have, in the past, been addressed by leading figures in radio drama writing and production, and are open to any aspiring writers in Sussex.

Series of short stories by local authors are also occasionally broadcast, but opportunities to contribute to these series, or to the radio play competition, are always well publicised by the station and authors are recommended to respond to such publicity rather than submit unsolicited work.

South and West

BBC South and West covers an area stretching from Gloucester to Guernsey and from Sussex to the Scilly Isles. It contains three regional television stations: BBC West, based in Bristol, BBC South West in Plymouth, and BBC South in Southampton. The Region also contains six local radio stations: BBC Radio Bristol, Cornwall, Devon, Solent, Jersey and Guernsey. Three more stations, Radio Dorset, Gloucestershire and Wiltshire, are due to go on air over the next two or three years.

The main production centre within the Region is in Bristol, where more than 600 staff are employed, in addition to others recruited on short-term contracts to work on specific projects. It possesses one large and one small television studio, and (excluding those of BBC Radio Bristol) four radio studios, one of which is acknowledged as among the best equipped drama studios in the world.

Network Television

Bristol is the base for the world-famous BBC Natural History Unit, which produces such series as *Wildlife on One*, with Sir David Attenborough, and *The Natural World* on BBC-2. It has also established its reputation through such major series as *Life on Earth* and *The Living Planet*. Many features are also produced in Bristol for the national networks, principally in the area of factual programmes. Documentary films and series form a major part of its output. The Department was, for example, responsible for the *Police* series on BBC-1 and has followed this with other observational documentaries. It also produces the popular *Antiques Roadshow* and *Whicker's World* series. Other programmes produced in Bristol include *Under Sail* and the discussion programme *Thinking Aloud*. Ideas for new feature series are welcome and all material should be addressed to the Head of Television Features, BBC South and West, Whiteladies Road, Bristol BS8 2LR.

BBC regional television in the South and West concentrates mainly on news and current affairs. The stations receive free-lance contributions from news agencies and in this way young journalists may get copy into news programmes although they are not trained in broadcasting. Individual contributions will only be accepted if the News Editor can be certain of the professional competence of the source. In short, regional television offers only limited opportunities for would-be writers.

Network Radio

Radio in Bristol, like television, reflects the area's 'specialisms' of natural history and antiques, but neither of these requires unsolicited contributions. Bristol also produces some editions of *Woman's Hour* and items with a West Country flavour are welcome.

Bristol contributes to all the radio drama series already described and the market is identical with that for drama department in London. Drama and feature programmes produced in Bristol are not restricted to local actors, and the cast may be drawn from all over the country. Regional overtones in the output are not essential, but authors living in the South and West will probably in any case be referred to Bristol if their work is felt to be of interest. Scripts rejected by London will not be considered in Bristol, and television and stage plays should not be submitted unless they have been readapted for radio by their authors. Adaptations are invariably commissioned from experienced writers, so should not be submitted unsolicited. *Morning Story*, to which Bristol contributes once a month, offers a good outlet for the new writer. Scripts, especially those with some regional link (e.g. with a West Country setting), should be submitted to Bristol rather than to London. Writers with original ideas can put forward suggestions for radio programmes that do not necessarily fit into any of the 'slots' already described. Drama scripts should be sent to Drama Producer (Radio) at Broadcasting House, Bristol. Other material intended for radio should be addressed to Head of Network Radio at Broadcasting House, Bristol.

BBC West

BBC West serves almost two million people in the West Country, through Avon, Somerset, Gloucestershire, Wiltshire and Dorset.

Its news magazine programme, *Points West*, is produced Monday to Friday and regularly attracts a large audience. Each weekday the newsroom also provides seven bulletins on BBC-1 – from *Breakfast Time* to after *The Nine O'Clock News*. A five-minute news and sport summary is transmitted on Saturdays.

BBC West's topical series *West on Two* goes out on BBC-2 on Friday evenings. It provides an opportunity for a longer look at issues affecting the West; it also provides time for a more easy-going approach in series such as Angela Rippon's *Day Out*, in which she visits locations of general interest.

BBC West programme makers have achieved success on the networks with programmes like *All Change at Evercreech Junction*, which also won the Royal Television Society award for the best regional programme, *Fans*, a picture of hero worship in the pop world, *Gold*, the story behind the Brinks-Mat robbery, and *It's Lineker for Barcelona*, an account of footballer Gary Lineker's first year in Spain.

BBC South West

BBC South West, based in Plymouth, serves Devon, Cornwall, the Channel Islands, Isles of Scilly and areas of Dorset and Somerset.

Its news magazine programme *Spotlight* – Monday to Friday – attracts, in its area, as big a following as some of the top ten network programmes. Like other regional stations it provides seven news bulletins each weekday on BBC-1 and a news and sports summary on Saturdays.

In addition to producing Friday night regional programmes covering everything from the arts to documentary features and news and current affairs, BBC South West also has a growing reputation for making network television programmes. Keith Floyd's 'gastronautic' programmes – which began as regional programmes – have established themselves as a national favourite, and *Waterfront*, a new magazine on maritime affairs, comes from Plymouth.

BBC South

From studios in Southampton, BBC South reports daily on

events that affect the lives of around four million people in an area which stretches along the coast from Brighton to Weymouth and as far inland as Salisbury, Newbury, Reading and Aldershot.

South Today, the nightly news magazine programme, is the station's 'flagship' and is consistently the best-watched news programme in the South. The newsroom which produces *South Today* also provides seven regional news bulletins for BBC-1 and, on Saturday afternoons, the latest news and sport.

Friday brings feature programmes on BBC-2. *South on Two Inquiry* keeps abreast of major current topics, the nature series *King's Country* was an award winner, Bob Wellings explored *Solent Way*, and *Painters* featured the work of local artists.

Some of the regional features have been successfully screened on the network. Others like a series on *Venture Capitalists* have been made specifically for the network.

Radio Bristol

Radio Bristol began broadcasting on 4 September 1970 – the first of twelve new BBC stations to be sanctioned following the original success of the two-year experiment in local broadcasting. It covers a very large geographical area encompassing the whole of the counties of Avon and Somerset, a large part of west Wiltshire, and smaller parts of south Gloucestershire and north Dorset. The main centre of broadcasting is in Tyndalls Park Road, Bristol, but the station also has manned studios in Kingsmead Square, Bath, to serve that area of Avon and West Wiltshire, and in Paul Street, Taunton, to cater for Somerset.

About one million people live in the heavily populated, northern half of the editorial area; in and around Bristol and Bath and the dormitory towns and villages. Industry and commerce are the major occupations in the urban areas, but there are another 500,000 people living in the country areas – a large number of whom are engaged in the farming industry. Tourism is another important industry and tends to overlap with agriculture these days, as more and more farms offer holiday accommodation as an extra side to their business.

Weston-super-Mare is the biggest attraction for holidaymakers, mainly from the Midlands and North, but there is pressure for more hotels in the cities as they become more attractive as tourist centres. Both Bristol and Bath have large and important universities, and Bristol Polytechnic is one of the largest and most comprehensive in the country. Its premises are scattered throughout the city, but there is also a large campus which is built on a 'green-field' site – close to the 32 link motorway with the M4.

One of Bristol's main advantages is its communications links, via the M4 to either London or Cardiff, and north and south on the M5 linking the Midlands and Exeter. British Rail's 125 diesel high-speed trains were also first introduced on the West region, linking Bristol with London in just over an hour.

Radio Bristol orginates more than eighty hours a week of general programmes, including a number of specialist music and minority interest programmes. In the main, however, the daily output is sequence programmes which mix news and current affairs with music, interviews and general interest features.

On Monday to Friday the station goes on air at 6.00 a.m. with *Morning West, Compass* from 9.00 a.m. till 12.30 p.m., the *Afternoon Show* from 12.30 p.m. until 3.00 p.m. and the *Teatime* programmes from 3.00 until 6.00 p.m. Both the mid-morning sequence and afternoon show are interested in offers of scripts, either for professional delivery or for delivery by the writer. Poetry also has its place and short stories are a regular feature of the *Afternoon Show*. Well-produced tapes and cassettes, as well as unsolicited scripts, can be sent to the Programme Organiser, at BBC Radio Bristol.

Radio Cornwall

BBC Radio Cornwall went on the air on 17 January 1983 – the same morning as breakfast television – and has consistently attracted the highest audience of any BBC mainland station in the years since then. There has always been a strong following for all forms of radio in Cornwall, but a local station that appeals to the powerful Cornish identity will always be a magnet.

Cornwall has always had a strong literary flavour: the Nobel Laureate William Golding is a Cornishman who has now returned to live in his homeland. Other resident writers range from John Le Carré to Charles Causley and Peter Redgrove.

Radio Cornwall has attempted to reflect this literary interest in its output. A competition to find new radio playwrights in the South West attracted scores of entries from Cornwall and six plays were eventually broadcast as a result of a joint enterprise with Radio Devon and Radio Bristol. There have also been short story competitions, usually most successful when they have had to conform to a particular theme. The radio station has also adapted Cornish books and stories – notably a series about the adventures of a nineteenth-century sailor under the title *Tales of a Cornish Mariner*. Plans for further series are under consideration.

Radio Cornwall always welcomes unsolicited material. The travel diaries of a nineteenth-century visitor to Cornwall proved to be very popular when they were adapted into a series for the breakfast programme, a good example of material coming from 'out of the blue'. Poems, particularly light verse, are broadcast regularly, though the station stipulates that the material should be by Cornish writers or on Cornish themes. Contributions should be sent to the Programme Organiser.

Radio Devon

BBC Radio Devon opened on 17 January 1983 – the same morning that Radio Cornwall and BBC Breakfast Television also took to the air. Radio Devon and Radio Cornwall replaced the last of the BBC's former regional services, based in Plymouth. Radio Devon serves the whole of one of the biggest counties in England, with a population of about a million. The station's main studios are based in Exeter, but programmes are also produced at the sub-base in Plymouth. District studios are also maintained in Barnstaple and Torbay.

The station now produces nearly ninety hours a week of local programmes, and has a staff of thirty full-time employees, as well as a number of part-time and contract staff.

During 1985 Radio Devon offered a short story competition and is likely to repeat the scheme from time to time. The winning entries were read by professionals. In 1986 Radio Devon organised a play-writing competition in conjunction with Radio Cornwall and Radio Bristol. Six winning plays were produced at what was then the Network Production Centre in Bristol, and were broadcast by all three stations.

Unsolicited cassettes and tapes are welcome, as well as scripts, which should be sent to the Programme Organiser. The station does pay for contributions but there is no regular outlet for short stories of a general nature. Material of specific local interest is more likely to interest the station, whether it be a short talk or a possible half-hour programme.

Radio Guernsey

BBC Radio Guernsey went on the air (along with its sister-station in Jersey) on 16 March 1982. Radio Guernsey is based at St Peter Port, Guernsey, and its programme output serves a population of approximately 60,000 in all the islands of the Bailiwick – i.e. Guernsey, Alderney, Sark and Herm. The population is divided into roughly one half working and one half non-working. The non-working population comprises retired people, housewives and school children. The working population is employed largely in the horticultural and agricultural industries (in particular, tomato-growing), the building industry and, the fastest growing trade – the banking and money business. Tourism is also an important feature in the Bailiwick's economy.

Radio Guernsey broadcasts seven hours a day of local material, including contributions from the community.

Local programming consists of sequences of news and information at breakfast time, and more leisurely daily programmes mid-morning and lunchtime comprising news, interviews, music, phone-ins, education and consumer material. The station would welcome contributions, both written and on tape, provided they have an immediate relevance to Guernsey and its sister islands. Material should be addressed to The Manager.

Radio Jersey

Radio Jersey has been on the air since March 1982 and broadcasts for an average of six hours per day – mainly news and current affairs relating to the island, but also includes general magazine material in its mid-morning programme.

Because of its size, the station does not include professional talks in its output or offer a market for unsolicited material. Potential contributors should contact the station before submitting scripts or programme ideas.

Radio Solent

BBC Radio Solent went on the air on 31 December 1970. It is one of the BBC's larger local stations covering parts of five counties – Hampshire, Wiltshire, Dorset, West Sussex and the Isle of Wight – a mixture of prosperous rural England with a large number of retired people and the light industrial, densely populated cities of Southampton and Portsmouth. The adult population of one and a half million is swollen considerably during the high summer by hundreds of thousands of visitors and at weekends by thousands of day trippers and yachtsmen who crowd the waters of the Solent. The audience also includes a large number of servicemen in the Royal Navy at Portsmouth.

The station transmits around ninety hours of locally-originated programmes each week, put together by a staff of thirty-two and a number of freelance journalists, presenters and programme assistants.

BBC Radio Solent's main aim is to provide local information entertainingly. This is done at breakfast-time in *Solent Today*, broadcast each weekday from 6.00 a.m. to 9.00 a.m., and at weekends in *The Location Quiz* – the station's longest running feature, which has been broadcast for more than fifteen years, and combines local knowledge and education in a quiz format where listeners set the clues to a location in the area.

A number of successful BBC paperback publications have sprung from programmes broadcast on Radio Solent, including two editions of *New Forest Walks* by Anne Marie Edwards and, by the same author, *In the Steps of Jane Austen* and *Discovering Hardy's Wessex*. These developed from what was originally intended to be a ten-minute talk, describing a walk through the New Forest, and the history of the ancient monuments, churches and other buildings in the area. Thus though the speaker's original fee was very modest the value of the 'spin-offs' proved to be substantial.

Radio Solent has encouraged writers and poets on a number of occasions since the station went on the air on New Year's Eve

1970, usually through competitions, run in conjunction with libraries in Hampshire and the Isle of Wight, which have formed part of long-running regular programmes on Radio Solent – not forming programmes in their own right. One-off stories, however, are not likely to be used, as the amount of good-quality material available is insufficient for a regular series and would prove too costly in terms of production effort. Scripts and other material should normally be sent to the Programme Organiser.

The National Regions

BBC Scotland, Wales and Northern Ireland are responsible (a) for producing and transmitting programmes to be seen and heard only within their respective countries and (b) for providing programmes for the networks. In Wales, Scotland and Northern Ireland the responsibility for the policy and content of programmes rests with their respective Broadcasting Councils, which are required, by the BBC's Charter, to bear in mind 'the distinctive culture, language, interests and tastes' of the countries concerned. This is achieved in the National Regions by means of additional, separate radio services (Radio Scotland, Radio nan Gaidheal, Radio Ulster, Radio Wales and Radio Cymru) most of which have small 'opt-out' stations providing localised variations. Radios 1, 2, 3 and 4 are the same in the National Regions as in England. In television, BBC-2 is the same as in England but in place of BBC-1 there is a different service, which includes regional programmes, though it also includes most BBC-1 programmes, shown either simultaneously or at a different time.

BBC Scotland

The BBC shares with the National Broadcasting Council for Scotland the responsibility for the policy and content of television programmes produced primarily for reception in Scotland, and of programmes on Radio Scotland, which is a different service from the networked Radio 4 heard in England, though with some programmes in common. The headquarters of BBC Scotland is in Glasgow, which possesses large-scale colour television facilities, and there are small television studios in Edinburgh, Aberdeen and Dundee. Inverness has a comprehensive radio centre with an output in Gaelic and English. Many of the programmes are specifically broadcast to the North and West, but the station also contributes in Gaelic and English to Radio Scotland. In television, BBC Scotland originates about ten hours of programmes a week for showing within Scotland and also makes regular and significant contributions to both BBC-1 and BBC-2, the volume of which is expanding. In drama, the requirement is for plays lasting for ninety, seventy-five or fifty minutes, which present some stimulating contemporary situation and have, if possible, a Scottish background, theme or characters. Historical costume drama is rarely required, as a stock of suitable scripts is already available, or will be produced by adaptations from books. All of Scotland's Drama output consists of plays, series and serials, intended for a network audience. New authors should submit a two- to three-page synopsis of the play, with detailed character notes, and may then be asked to write some specimen scenes.

So far as radio is concerned, Scotland contributes to all the networked slots and series described under the 'Drama' heading earlier in this book. These may be of any of the standard lengths and of all intellectual levels. Policy is to seek plays reflecting contemporary Scotland. At the same time dramatic merit rather than any degree of 'Scottishness' remains the final criterion. Material which explores the freedoms and challenges of the medium of Sound is especially welcome. A complementary output is maintained on Radio Scotland. Contributions, again of varying lengths, are invited – as is other work, in poetry or prose, conceived for the medium.

Radio and Television scripts should be sent respectively to the Senior Drama Producer (Radio) at Broadcasting House, Edinburgh, and the Head of Television Drama, Scotland, at Broadcasting House, Glasgow.

Scotland is also interested in receiving suggestions for radio and television documentary programmes of Scottish interest, preferably submitted in the form of a treatment, though ideas will also be considered. Material should be addressed to the Head of Television, Scotland, at Broadcasting House, Glasgow. In the case of light entertainment, television scripts of the situation comedy type lasting thirty minutes can be considered. Few radio light-entertainment scripts are used by Radio Scotland, but suitable scripts, thirty minutes in length, may be offered. Scripts should be sent to the Head of Comedy at Broadcasting House, Glasgow.

Talks should preferably be fifteen minutes long or twenty minutes for those intended for concert intervals and may cover almost any subject, though nostalgic personal recollections and experiences of travel are less likely to be acceptable. Some degree of personal involvement in the subject, or specialist knowledge, is usually looked for. New writers for radio are advised in the first instance to submit an idea, not a script. Short stories, preferably fifteen minutes in length, are also required, provided they are written by an author living in Scotland. The qualities looked for are simplicity of theme and a relatively small amount of dialogue, with a minimum of different 'voices'. Both talks and short stories should be addressed to Talks and Features Department at Broadcasting House, Edinburgh.

Television and radio scripts in the Gaelic language are welcome, for in spite of the recent increase in Gaelic publications, broadcasting still provides the main outlet in the language for creative writing and ideas. The output covers a wide range of programmes and there is always a need for material, particularly for radio. Talks, features, plays, documentaries, poetry and songs are all broadcast on Radio Scotland. Talks can be of any length from a few minutes to fifteen, and features, plays and documentaries can vary from thirty to forty-five minutes and, exceptionally, sixty minutes; but items of outstanding merit will be considered regardless of these limits. Material for a particular date should be submitted four to six months in advance, depending on the degree of preparation involved. Scripts and ideas should be sent to the Head of Gaelic Broadcasting at Broadcasting House, Glasgow.

BBC Wales

BBC Wales is the largest BBC operation outside London. It is the only part of the BBC's domestic services which has to serve a bilingual population (the Welsh language, which is spoken by about twenty per cent of the population of Wales, was given 'equal status' to English in Wales by Act of Parliament in 1967). Welsh-language programmes are designed to be seen and heard only in Wales, while programmes in English are made both for the BBC's UK networks and for transmission only to Wales. BBC Wales has its headquarters at Llandaff in Cardiff which has excellent radio studios and a newsroom together with two television studios, a large one for major productions and a small one mainly for news, current affairs and magazine programmes. The North Wales headquarters in Bangor provides about half the output of Radio Cymru, but also has limited television contribution facilities. Finally there is a small radio operation in Swansea and the first Radio Wales opt-out station, Radio Clwyd, is based in Mold in North-East Wales; the second, Radio Gwent, serves the South-East and is based in Cwmbran.

Television

BBC Wales's programmes for the BBC-1 and BBC-2 networks include documentaries, music, drama and light entertainment and amount to about one hour per week on average. Its opt-out programmes in English for Wales are broadcast only on BBC-Wales television and consist mainly of news, current affairs, sport and music; these programmes occupy about seven hours per week of air-time. The largest segment of television output is in the Welsh language, amounting to about ten hours a week, for transmission on S4C.

The programmes which the BBC contributes to the Welsh Fourth Channel (S4C) are commissioned, planned, produced and financed on precisely the same terms as programmes intended for showing on BBC Wales. All categories of production are covered – drama, light entertainment, children's programmes, documentaries, features, news (but not current affairs, by agreement with S4C), sport, outside broadcast events, religion, music and education. There is a substantial output of drama in both Welsh, for S4C, and English, for BBC Video. Recent English output has included *That Uncertain Feeling* and *Shadowlands*. Plays of thirty, fifty and seventy-five minutes are all welcome. Ideas for serials, which may run for any number of episodes up to a maximum of thirteen or fourteen, will be considered and in this case the full script of the first episode should be offered, with a detailed synopsis of the rest. Ideas for series (as defined earlier in this booklet) will be considered and here the idea alone should be submitted in the first instance. Suggestions for thrillers and comedy material will be especially welcome. BBC Wales produces a number of adaptations of novels and short stories, both in Welsh, for S4C, and in English, for itself. In this case enquiry should be made before submitting a script to ensure that the story concerned has not already been adapted, or rejected as unsuitable for adaptation. Children's Programmes Department, with a varied television output, requires scripts and ideas for programmes in Welsh: programmes can be submitted in English for final scripts in Welsh. There are plans, not yet finalised, for some output in English. Film documentaries on subjects related to Wales are made from time to time; ideas from established writers will be given consideration within the General Programmes Department.

Light Entertainment material is welcome in both languages in the form of quick sketches lasting only three or four minutes, very brief 'black-out' sketches, and ideas for quizzes and panel games. Ideas for situation comedy series are also welcome, normally, but not essentially, in a Welsh setting and with a limited number of characters, not usually exceeding four or five 'residents': A full script of the first episode is required, with some indication of the ways in which the situation might be exploited in subsequent programmes.

Radio Wales

Programmes for Wales

Radio Wales produces some eighty hours a week of programmes broadcast on medium wave and also relays some programmes from Radios 2 and 4. All its output is in English. All types of programme are produced, including news bulletins, topical magazines, light entertainment, religious programmes, talks and documentaries, and a small amount of drama. Scripts and ideas should be submitted to the Editor, Radio Wales, at Broadcasting House, Llandaff.

Contributions to the Network

BBC Wales's contribution to the BBC's network radio consists of programmes originally made for Radio Wales and also of others specifically produced for the networks. *Morning Story* and *Story Time*, which mainly carried adaptations, both offer opportunities to the writer, but some relevance to Wales is necessary. For *Woman's Hour*, though most contributions are commissioned, unsolicited scripts will be considered. BBC Wales has also contributed talks, normally of fifteen minutes, features and documentaries to the networks. These cover the whole range of topics, usually with some Welsh connection. Drama is mainly produced for Radio 3 or Radio 4, the requirements being as indicated in the main Drama Department entry earlier in this booklet, although the station also has its own Drama season of plays intended initially for transmission in Wales only. The writer or his work should have some connection with Wales. As there is only one radio drama producer based in Cardiff, who receives several hundred manuscripts a year – though only a few of these are eventually produced – there is bound to be some delay before unsolicited manuscripts can be read. In the case of an unestablished writer, only a complete script can be considered. Features and documentaries, normally of forty-five or sixty minutes, are also produced in Wales. Both contemporary and historical subjects are of interest. In the first instance a two- or three-page outline should be submitted.

BBC Wales has organised a number of weekend seminars at a country house outside Cardiff, attended by about fifty people, which cover writing for both radio and television, with the chief emphasis on drama. Most of those attending are unestablished writers and attendance is not restricted to writers resident in Wales, though they tend to predominate. Most of the proceedings consist of discussions led by established writers and members of BBC Drama staff. Enquiries should be addressed to Head of Drama, Drama Department, at Llandaff.

Radio Cymru

Radio Cymru has a staff of about thirty, divided between Cardiff, Bangor and Swansea. It broadcasts exclusively in Welsh, producing a total output of about seventy-five hours a week, though when not on the air its wavelength (on FM) normally carries Radio 4 as a 'sustaining' service. It is extensively patronised by the Welsh-speaking population. Since it came on the air in 1979, Radio Cymru has created a whole new market for Welsh writers but the Editor is always interested in hearing from potential contributors, who need not have radio-writing experience, or be resident in Wales, though they must, of course, be Welsh-speaking. Contributions are paid for at the prevailing rate. The station's style is closest to that of Radio 4, but much of the output is built round a magazine format and it contains every type of material, including news and current affairs, music (including 'pop' songs in Welsh), drama, light entertainment, features, documentaries, religious programmes, sport, outside broadcasts and children's programmes.

News material is contributed by staff members or established freelances and does not offer any market for other outside contributors. The main magazine programmes which use scripted material are, *Merched yn Bennaf (Mainly for Women)*, which uses the same type of material as *Woman's Hour*, and *Rhwng Gwyl A Gwaith (Between Rest and Work)*, a Sunday evening magazine programme which regularly features scripted talks, mainly of six or seven minutes, with a preference for non-topical subjects. In the field of drama a substantial market exists for series, thrillers, adaptations and single plays. The requirement for single plays is usually for forty-five minutes and for adaptations episodes of thirty minutes, though other lengths may be accepted. The action need not take place in Wales. For series and serials the usual requirement is for four to six episodes of thirty minutes.

Radio Cymru also regularly features situation comedy and the demand here is for thirty-minute scripts. From a new writer a complete script would normally be required, and if this seemed likely to extend to a whole series he might then be asked to submit a proposed treatment for other episodes, up to a maximum of six, using the same characters. In the Light Entertainment area Radio Cymru already carries a number of panel-games but ideas for others, which need not necessarily involve audience participation, are welcome, for programmes up to thirty minutes in length.

A regular programme for children and teenagers, *Ribidires*, is broadcast on Saturday mornings from 8.15 to 9 a.m. This includes a short episode, of ten minutes or less, of a serial, or a self-contained story or comic drama. Would-be contributors should submit one complete episode and some indication of how the story would develop through a run of up to ten. Original works are preferred but suggestions for the adaptation of existing stories will be considered.

Radio Cymru is not in the market for unsolicited scripts for religious programmes, for which all material is commissioned by the staff. Nor are unsolicited contributions sought for agricultural programmes. General enquiries and contributions for which no other address is given above, should be addressed to The Editor, Radio Cymru, Broadcasting House, Llandaff.

BBC Northern Ireland

Television opt-out programmes in Northern Ireland amount to approximately six and a half hours per week. Of this, more than two hours is taken up by the nightly opt-out News and information magazine. Current Affairs, outside broadcasts, film documentaries, music and the other arts, schools, farming, sport and religious broadcasting, form the basis of the remainder of the regional output.

There is a market for several television plays each year for the BBC-1 and BBC-2 networks. These plays can be made entirely in a studio, or on location using film cameras or an outside broadcast unit, or they can be made with a combination of these facilities. Scripts for plays should be sent to the Head of Programmes at Broadcasting House, Belfast.

The Schools department commissions scripts and enquiries should be directed to Head of Schools Broadcasting. Ideas for television documentaries are welcome, and may also be submitted, in the form of a synopsis and proposed treatment, to the Head of Programmes, at the above address.

In Radio, the market is more substantial. Radio Ulster, the BBC network for Northern Ireland, was launched in January 1975, and is an additional service to Radios 1, 2, 3 and 4. Radio Ulster now provides about seventy hours of locally originated programmes each week. Radio Foyle, an opt-out service from Radio Ulster for the Londonderry area, mounts about twenty hours a week of locally originated material. It has been broadcasting since September 1979. Ideas for new programmes, whether for single programmes or series, are welcomed, but are most likely to be accepted if worked out in detail and accompanied by sample scripts. These should be submitted to the Deputy Head of Programmes, at the BBC in Belfast, or, where appropriate, to the Manager of Radio Foyle, P.O. Box 927, Rock Road, Londonderry.

In addition to providing Radio Ulster and Radio Foyle, BBC staff in Northern Ireland service the four main BBC radio networks. There is a regular demand for plays suitable for offering to the Radio 3 and Radio 4 networks. In the main, these should reflect Ireland and the Irish. There is also a market for fifteen-minute short stories (about 2200 words). Enquiries about plays should be directed to the Drama Producer, and short stories, poetry and other new writing should be submitted to the Senior Producer, Arts Programmes Radio, at the BBC in Belfast. It is recommended that writers and authors should watch and listen to the output from the Northern Ireland studios and study the range of programmes made by reading the Northern Ireland edition of *Radio Times*.

The BBC External Services

The External Services are an integral part of the BBC, operating under the same Charter as the rest of the Corporation, but financed by a government grant-in-aid and not from licence revenue. The government also lays down the languages in which broadcasts shall be made, and the number of hours each service will be on the air, but has no responsibility for the content of programmes. Some programmes originating on the domestic services are repeated for the overseas audience and from time to time the External Services may provide domestic radio or television with expert assistance or material on particular areas overseas. In general, however, the External Services and domestic services can be regarded as essentially separate. The External Services broadcast to countries outside the United Kingdom, their output consisting on the one hand of the World Service, which is broadcast in English throughout the twenty-four hours and is directed to all parts of the world, and on the other of services to particular countries or areas, both in English and in thirty-eight other languages. Apart from English by Radio and Television, which is dealt with separately later, the External Services broadcast solely on radio and do not make television programmes. A very high proportion of the output of all services consists of news and current affairs programmes. These offer little scope for unsolicited contributions from freelance writers, but there are sometimes openings in the following fields.

World Service

This is a fully comprehensive radio network including news, current affairs, documentary features, talks, drama, music and programmes on the arts, finance, industry, science, agriculture, religion and sport. The majority of programmes are prepared internally or commissioned from established freelance writers, but new contributors are considered if they can supply evidence of expert knowledge and professional skill. Application, by preliminary letter, should be made to Assistant Head of Productions, World Service, BBC, Bush House, London.

Central Current Affairs Talks

This Department supplies commentaries and analytical talks of approximately 500 words on international affairs, economic and political subjects for broadcasting in English and for translation into other languages. Contributors should have specialist knowledge of their subject with an ability to put it across to an educated but non-specialist audience overseas. Scripts are commissioned after consultation. Enquiries should be made to Head of Central Talks and Features, BBC, Bush House.

Central Talks and Features

This Department produces a regular flow of scripts for the language services to translate and broadcast. Opportunities for freelancers are limited but offers of short talks (about 500 words) on events in the social and cultural life of Britain can be made to the Editor, Features and Topical Reports, BBC, Bush House. There is also some scope for talks on scientific and industrial matters, ideally concerning developments in the UK which are appropriate to worldwide audiences: these should be addressed to Editor, Science, Industry and Export Unit, BBC, Bush House. Writers on such topics are expected to have an expertise in the appropriate field. In both the topical and the scientific areas, it is essential to approach the subject in such a way that it is of interest and relevance to an audience which cannot be assumed to be familiar with British institutions or the British way of life.

Foreign-Language Services

The foreign-language services offer limited opportunities for freelancers, who should preferably be able to broadcast in the appropriate foreign language, for talks dealing with topics of specific interest to audiences in that language. Offers should be made to the Organiser of the appropriate language service at Bush House.

English by Radio and Television

The English by Radio and Television Department provides courses in English for foreign students. Its radio courses are broadcast on most of the BBC's External Services and many programmes are also distributed free, as transcriptions. Programmes are divided into those intended for beginners and those for more advanced students. The former usually consist of a dialogue scene or other material, in English, together with an instructional commentary in the language of the country at which the programme is aimed. Scripts are normally written initially in English, the appropriate parts being later translated or adapted. The courses for intermediate and advanced students are wholly in English and range from lessons illustrating everyday colloquial idiom, many of them presented in serial-story form, to discussions on style and usage and selections of extracts from the work of established writers, with a linguistic commentary. There is also a magazine programme which includes short topical talks on the use and study of English in different parts of the world, and there are occasional special courses on such subjects as the English of commerce or of science and technology. Apart from talks, most scripted material is read by actors.

To write for *English by Radio*, contributors must have personal knowledge of the problems of teaching English as a foreign language, coupled with the ability to put this knowledge in a suitable radio form. Scripts are generally bought outright, but when, as sometimes happens, a course is reissued commercially in recorded form, the author may be invited to prepare an accompanying textbook on a royalty basis.

The *English by Television* courses are made on film for showing by foreign television stations, and the scripts are mostly written by professional television scriptwriters working in close co-operation with language specialists.

Publications giving details of the current output are available from the address below, to which suggestions for series and programme items, or offers to contribute to existing programmes, should be sent: Head of English by Radio and Television, BBC, P.O. Box 76, Bush House, London WC2B 4PH.

How to Submit Material

Submitting Scripts

Scripts and all similar documents should be sent to the addresses stated, with a brief covering letter. The name and address of the sender should be given on the script, together with an indication of the content and its approximate length in minutes when read aloud, e.g. 'Nursing in New Guinea, a talk for radio, 4 minutes (650 words).' Where plays are concerned, it is helpful if a list of characters is given on the title-page, with, in the case of television, a list of the studio sets and film sequences. Manuscripts *must* be typewritten, on one side of the paper only, preferably on A4 paper. Specimen layouts are shown on pp. 96–97. A stamped addressed envelope should be enclosed for the return of unused contributions.

Submitting Tapes

Those departments willing to consider tape-recorded material have already been indicated. The BBC handles many thousands of tapes a year, and it is therefore essential for all tapes to be clearly labelled, with the relevant details (subject, name and address of sender, the tape speed, and the length in minutes), on the box. Tapes for listening only should preferably be submitted on cassette. Tapes for possible broadcasting should be on reel-to-reel tape. Tapes of speech can be considered if the general quality is good, at speeds of 15, $7\frac{1}{2}$ and $3\frac{3}{4}$ i.p.s., tapes of music at 15 or $7\frac{1}{2}$ i.p.s. Tapes at slower speeds are not suitable for broadcasting. In the case of tapes carrying speech, a typed transcript should be enclosed.

The BBC does not accept any responsibility for the safe keeping or return of unsolicited scripts and tapes.

Specimen Page of a Television Script (Drama)

15. INT. A PUB IN CHELSEA. NIGHT

> (JOHN AND EDWARD ARE DRINKING AT
> A TABLE)

EDWARD: You've done that? Put a pivate
detective on to her?

JOHN: Yes.

EDWARD: I hate to see this happening to
you two. You and Lisa have been my friends
for years.

JOHN: (DISTRAUGHT) I've got to find out! Who
it is my wife's been seeing! Who's been...

TELECINE:

EXT. Belmont Road.
NIGHT.

Private detective in
car, parked opposite
an apartment block.
His POV.

A door opens. LISA
and MAX come out. He
shuts the door. They
walk down the road to
a car and drive off.

The detective writes
something in his
notebook.

END TELECINE.

16. INT. MAX'S OFFICE IN THE CITY. DAY.

> (MAX ALONE AT HIS DESK. THE INTERCOM
> BUZZES. HE PRESSES A SWITCH)

SECRETARY: (INTERCOM) Assistant Manager to
see you, sir.

MAX: Send him in.

> (STILL ON MAX. WE HEAR THE DOOR OPEN
> AND SOMEONE ENTER.)

> John! Come in. Tell me about the
> Maryland business.

(PAUSE)

> What's that you've got...No...Look...

> (ON JOHN, WHO HAS A REVOLVER IN HIS HAND
> POINTED AT MAX.)

17. INT. JOHN AND LISA'S FRONT ROOM. DAY.

> (LISA ALONE. SHE SITS ON THE SOFA
> READING A FASHION MAGAZINE, AND SIPS
> A GLASS OF WINE. SHE GLANCES AT THE
> PHONE FROM TIME TO TIME. IT DULY RINGS.
> SHE QUICKLY PUTS DOWN THE MAGAZINE
> AND THE GLASS, GOES TO THE PHONE, PICKS
> UP THE RECEIVER.)

LISA: (BRIGHTLY) Yes?

N.B. Simple descriptions of characters when they first appear.
Eg. JOHN TAYLOR, A SALES MANAGER, EARLY FORTIES. HIS WIFE LISA,
EARLY THIRTIES. MAX JOHNSON, A COMPANY CHAIRMAN, MID-FORTIES.

96

Specimen Page of a Radio Script (Drama)

SCENE 10:   (A LONELY COUNTRY ROAD IN MIDWINTER. A LIGHT
EXTERIOR. NIGHT.   WIND IS BLOWING. IN THE DISTANCE, A DOG BARKS)

1. ARTHUR: (Close to mic) I hate him. I really hate him.
May his teeth ache and his eyes hurt in his head.
I hope his budgie dies.

                (DISTANT, APPROACHING BOOTS CLOP AND SCRAPE
ON THE METALLED ROAD. A TUNELESS WHISTLING
ACCOMPANIES THEM)

2. ARTHUR: (Close) Who's that? Don't tell me he's coming now.
It's past ten-thirty.

                (FOOTSTEPS NEARER)

3. ARTHUR: (Calling) Is that you, Murdo?

                (FOOTSTEPS STOP)

4. ARTHUR: Don't muck about. I'm freezing. Murdo?

                (NO REPLY)

5. ARTHUR: Oh, come on. I've been here for hours!

6. MOSCROP: (A little away) Don't make so much noise, Fat man.

7. ARTHUR: What? You're not Murdo. Who is it?

8. MOSCROP: The recording angel, Arthur. Your last trump.

                (A PISTOL SHOT, UNNATURALLY LOUD. AS IT'S
ECHOES DIE, THERE IS THE FLUTTERING OF A
FLOCK OF PIGEONS)

SCENE 11:   (LORD ABERFALDY'S ESTATE. THE PIGEONS FLY
EXTERIOR. DAY.   AWAY. APPLAUSE)

1 ABERFALDY: (Middle distance) Oh! good shot, Moscrop!
Army trainin'. Always shows.

2. MOSCROP: (Close. To himself) Doesn't it just, old darling.
Compost Street Comprehensive, actually: and too
young for National Service. But the shooting
gallery on Southend Pier can work wonders.

3 ABERFALDY: (Calling) Everybody back to the house, now!
Tiffin time! Come on!

                (A GENERAL MURMER OF PLEASURE, AND THE
GATHERING UP OF GUNS)

4. MOSCROP: Coming, my lord. Coming. (quietly) As the
actress said to the... oh, God I don't even amuse
myself. Is it worth it, I ask. Is it honestly
worth it? Here I stand, up to the boot tops in
life-enobled muck, potting away at pigeons with a gun
that could have been the price of a house in my
young days - and in the company of seven superannuated
stockbrokers without a chin between them. Not to
mention the noble lord. Well, yes, that's right: let's
not mention the noble lord. It might just spoil what
was otherwise becoming an utterly unmemorable day.

                (DISTANT DOGS BARKING. LAUGHTER)

Coming, my lord. Coming!

Some Useful Books

The most comprehensive guide to the services and previous year's output of the BBC is the *BBC Annual Report and Accounts*, published annually by the BBC.

The 1988 edition costs £4.50 and is available from any BBC bookshop or from major booksellers.

Television and Radio

The inclusion of a title on this list does not imply that the BBC endorses the contents, nor does the exclusion of a book carry any derogatory implication. In addition to the title shown, would-be writers may find it helpful to consult some of the many published television and radio scripts of previous drama and light entertainment programmes. Some are available in local libraries and from booksellers and all titles which are in print can be ordered, post-free, from Samuel French Ltd, 52 Fitzroy Street, London W1P 6JR (01–387–9373).

Television and general

Cooke, Brian *Writing comedy for television* Methuen, paperback 1983.

Edgar, David (et al.) *Ah! mischief: the writer and television* Faber, 1982.

Griffiths, Stuart *How plays are made* Heinemann Educational, paperback 1982.

Hilliard, Robert L. *Writing for television and radio* Focal Press, 1976.o.p.

Hulke, Malcolm *Writing for television* Black, n.e. 1984.

Maloney, Martin and Rubenstein, P. M. *Writing for the media* Prentice-Hall, 1980.

Paice, Eric *The way to write for television* Elm Tree Books, cased and paperback, 1981.

Self, David *Television drama: an introduction* Macmillan, cased and paperback, 1984.

Swain, Dwight V. *Film scriptwriting: a practical manual* Focal Press, n.e. 1982.

Willis, Edgar E. *Writing scripts for television, radio and film* Holt, Rinehart and Winston, n.e. 1981.

Radio

Dunbar, Janet *The radio talk: a practical study of the art and craft of talks broadcasting* Harrap, 1954.o.p.

Dunbar, Janet *Writing for radio* Foyles, 1954.

Gielgud, Val *The right way to radio playwriting* Rolls House Publishing Co., 1948.

Hilliard, Robert L. *Radio broadcasting: an introduction to the sound medium* Longman, 1985.

McWhinnie, Donald *The art of radio* Faber, 1959.

Sieveking, Lance *The stuff of radio* Cassell, 1934.

BBC Addresses

Corporate Headquarters
Broadcasting House, Portland Place, London W1A 1AA

Television
BBC Television Centre, Wood Lane, London W12 7RJ
Threshold House, 65–69 Shepherd's Bush Green, London W12 7RJ
Lime Grove Studios, Lime Grove, London W12 7RJ
Kensington House, Richmond Way, London W14 0AX
BBC Elstree Centre, Clarendon Road, Borehamwood, Herts WD6 1JF

Radio
Broadcasting House, Portland Place, London W1A 1AA

Educational Broadcasting
Television:
Schools – Head of School Broadcasting, Television, Villiers House, The Broadway, London W5 2PA
Continuing Education – Head of Continuing Education, Television, Villiers House, The Broadway, London W5 2PA
Radio:
Schools – Head of School Broadcasting Radio, 3 Portland Place, London W1A 1AA
Continuing Education – Head of Continuing Education, Radio, Henry Wood House, 3 and 6 Langham Place, London W1A 1AA

Religious Broadcasting
Television:
Head of Religious Broadcasting, BBC Television Centre, Wood Lane, London W12 7RJ
Radio:
Head of Religious Programmes, Radio, The Langham, Portland Place, London W1A 1AA

English Regions and Local Radio

BBC Midlands
Pebble Mill, Birmingham B5 7QQ

Local radio stations:

BBC Radio Derby   56 St Helen's Street, Derby DE1 3HY

BBC Radio Leicester   Epic House, Charles Street, Leicester LE1 3SH

BBC Radio Lincolnshire   Radio Buildings, Newport, Lincoln LN1 3DF

BBC Radio Nottingham   York House, Mansfield Road, Nottingham NG1 3JB

BBC Radio Shropshire   2/4 Boscobel Drive, Shrewsbury, Shropshire SY1 3TT

BBC Radio Stoke   Cheapside, Hanley, Stoke-on-Trent, Staffordshire ST1 1JJ

BBC Radio WM   Pebble Mill Road, Birmingham B5 7SD

BBC North East
Broadcasting House,   54 New Bridge Street, Newcastle upon Tyne, NE1 8AA
Broadcasting Centre,   Woodhouse Lane, Leeds LS2 9PX

Local radio stations:

BBC Radio Cleveland   Broadcasting House, Newport Road, Middlesbrough, Cleveland TS1 5DG

BBC Radio Humberside   63 Jameson Street, Hull HU1 3NU

BBC Radio Leeds   Broadcasting House, Woodhouse Lane, Leeds LS2 9PN

BBC Radio Newcastle   Broadcasting Centre, Barrack Road, Fenham, Newcastle upon Tyne NE99 1RN

BBC Radio Sheffield   Ashdell Grove, 60 Westbourne Road, Sheffield SI0 2QU

BBC Radio York   20 Bootham Row, York YO3 7BR

BBC North West
New Broadcasting House, Oxford Road, Manchester M60 1SJ

Local radio stations:

BBC Radio Cumbria   Hilltop Heights, London Road, Carlisle, Cumbria CA1 2NA

BBC Radio Lancashire   King Street, Blackburn, Lancashire BB2 2EA

BBC Radio Manchester   New Broadcasting House, Oxford Road, Manchester M60 1SJ

BBC Radio Merseyside   55 Paradise Street, Liverpool L1 3BP

BBC South and East
BBC Elstree Centre, Clarendon Road, Borehamwood, Herts WD6 1JF

Local radio stations:

BBC Radio Bedfordshire   P.O. Box 476, Hastings Street, Luton, Bedfordshire

BBC Radio Cambridgeshire   Broadcasting House, Hills Road, Cambridge CB2 1LD

BBC Radio Essex   198 New London Road, Chelmsford, Essex CM2 9XB

BBC Radio Kent   Sun Pier, Chatham, Kent ME4 4EZ

BBC Radio London   35a Marylebone High Street, London W1A 4LG

BBC Radio Norfolk   Norfolk Tower, Surrey Street, Norwich NR1 3PA

BBC Radio Northampton   Abington Street, Northampton NN1 2BE

BBC Radio Oxford   242–254 Banbury Road, Oxford OX2 7DW

BBC Radio Sussex   Marlborough Place, Brighton, Sussex BN1 1TU

BBC South and West
Broadcasting House, Whiteladies Road, Clifton, Bristol BS8 2LR
South Western House, Canute Road, Southampton, SO9 1PF
Broadcasting House, Seymour Road, Mannamead, Plymouth PL3 5BD

Local radio stations:

BBC Radio Bristol   3 Tyndalls Park Road, Bristol BS8 1PP

BBC Radio Cornwall   Phoenix Wharf, Truro, Cornwall TR1 1UA

BBC Radio Devon   St David's Hill, Exeter, Devon EX4 4DB

BBC Radio Guernsey   Commerce House, Les Banques, St Peter Port, Guernsey, Channel Islands

BBC Radio Jersey   Broadcasting House, Rouge Bouillon, St Helier, Jersey

BBC Radio Solent   South Western House, Canute Road, Southampton SO9 4PJ

The National Regions

BBC Scotland

Glasgow
Broadcasting House, Queen Margaret Drive, Glasgow G12
  8DG
Edinburgh
Broadcasting House, 5 Queen Street, Edinburgh EH2 1JF
Aberdeen
Broadcasting House, Beechgrove Terrace, Aberdeen AB9 2ZT
Dundee
12/13 Dock Street, Dundee

Community Stations:

BBC Highland   7 Culduthel Road, Inverness IV2 4AD
BBC Radio nan Gaidheal (Radio nan Eilean)   Rosebank,
  Church Street, Stornoway
BBC Radio Orkney   Castle Street, Kirkwall
BBC Radio Shetland   Brentham House, Lerwick, Shetland
  ZE1 0LR
BBC Radio Solway   Elmbank, Lovers' Walk, Dumfries, DG1
  1NZ
BBC Radio Tweed   Municipal Buildings, High Street, Selkirk,
  TD7 4BU

BBC Wales

Cardiff
Broadcasting House, Llantrisant Road, Llandaff, Cardiff CF5
  2YQ
Bangor
Bron Castell, High Street, Bangor, North Wales, LL57 1YU
Swansea
32 Alexandra Road, Swansea SA1 5DZ

Community Stations:

BBC Radio Clwyd   The Old School House, Glanrafon Road,
  Mold CH7 1PA
BBC Radio Gwent   Powys House, Cwmbran, Gwent NP44
  1YF

BBC Northern Ireland

Broadcasting House, 25–27 Ormeau Avenue, Belfast, 2, BT2
  8HQ
BBC Radio Foyle, P.O. Box 927, Rock Road, Londonderry

The External Services

P.O. Box 76, Bush House, Strand, London WC2B 4PH